"*The Hero's Mask* tells the story of children becoming heroes! It will inspire all who read it to face and overcome challenges with courage and bravery. *The Hero's Mask* is not about what has happened to you but who you can become. *The Hero's Mask Guidebook* combines research on the impact of trauma with a magical unfolding of the individual uniqueness and beauty of each child. It integrates theory, knowledge, and evidence-based practice with a soul depth that transcends the moment and calls us to be our 'best' selves to children. It provides a sacred pathway for child, parent, and adult healing."
James Henry, Ph.D. Professor of Social Work and Project Director, Children's Trauma Assessment Center, Western Michigan University.

"In the tradition of Joseph Campbell, George Lucas, and J.K. Rowling, Dr. Kagan uses the stories of heroes to illustrate how children can go through difficult times, learn from past mistakes, find strength in friendship, cope with the fear, discomfort, and paralysis of traumatic reminders, and become heroes in their own lives. He also illustrates in very practical ways how adults can nurture a child's inner resilience by showing grace and compassion, guiding them to shape their own narrative and make heroic choices.

In *The Hero's Mask*, Dr. Kagan tells a story that children will love, full of mystery and friendship, bullies and heroism. Through that story children can relate to a hero in Carrie, whose relationships help her to overcome her fears and understand the strength she and her friends have to make a difference in other's lives. Through Carrie's story, children can understand the power of connection and engagement as paths towards healing and heroism."

Jane Halladay Goldman, Ph.D., Director, Service Systems Program, UCLA-Duke University National Center for Child Traumatic Stress.

"*The Hero's Mask* is an engaging and timely novel about the impact of traumatic loss on children and much of what it takes for them to heal: good friends, nurturing adults, cultural wisdom, personal courage—and the power of storytelling itself. The companion *Guidebook* is a rich resource for caregivers, teachers, and counselors wanting to engage in deeper understanding and the difficult conversations that can support children through these toughest times."
Martha B. Straus, Ph.D., Professor, Antioch University and author of *Treating Trauma in Adolescents: Development, Attachment, and the Therapeutic Relationship.*

"In his novel, *The Hero's Mask*, Dr. Kagan beautifully demonstrates the profound power of connection in promoting healing and resilience. Through his characters and the theme of a hero's journey, he is able to bring the thematic of loss, human stress and the role of relationship to life in a context that is relatable to young people and the caregivers who support them. This novel along with the practical guidebook for parents and professionals is a unique tool written by someone who has clearly dedicated a career to understanding trauma, attachment, resilience and young people! Youth serving systems, families and children alike will benefit from this approach."
Kristine M. Kinniburgh, LCSW, Director of Trauma Services, Justice Resource Institute Connecticut, National trauma trainer and consultant, The Trauma Center at JRI. ARC Co-Developer and Co-author of *Treating traumatic stress in children and adolescents; How to foster resilience through attachment, self-regulation, and competency* (Guilford Press).

"*The Hero's Mask* is a very engaging, age-appropriate, and inspiring novel for middle grade children, especially for those who have experienced traumatic losses, bullying, disengaged parents and harsh authority figures. The central characters are multi-dimensional and relatable, and the narrative moves forward in an

adept, fast-paced manner that will engage most young readers. *The Hero's Mask* and the accompanying *Guidebook* represent a significant contribution to an understanding of children's trauma and actions that can be taken to reduce and resolve trauma."
Cheryl Lanktree, Ph.D., Adolescent Trauma Training Center, Keck School of Medicine, University of Southern California.

"For children and young teens who are feeling a lot of big emotions and are struggling to be understood, follow Carrie, the "hero" of *The Hero's Mask*, as she puts the feelings shared by so many others into words. This novel beautifully describes the way stress and trauma can show up in our bodies and affect our relationships with family and peers. Young readers learn with Carrie as she begins to connect the dots between her thoughts, feelings, and behaviors–to change the direction of her own story for the better.

The Hero's Mask is a great resource for schools that illustrates what students are really experiencing, how this affects their ability to learn and their behavior in the classroom, and the transformative role that educators can play. The accompanying Guidebook provides educators with a framework for understanding trauma-informed schools, as well as a structured approach for using *The Hero's Mask* with students in the classroom."
Jenifer Maze, PhD, Deputy Director, UCLA-Duke University National Center for Child Traumatic Stress.

"In writing *The Hero's Mask* and *Helping Children with Traumatic Stress*, Dr. Kagan offers a gift to children and families who have experienced trauma and to the caregivers, educators, and therapists who support these families. *The Hero's Mask* works as a standalone piece of literature with its well-developed characters and salient themes of interpersonal, community, and cultural adversity, trauma, and loss. Through 11-year-old Carrie and the other children and adults in her life, many readers will identify with the somatic, emotional, and behavioral experiences associated with trauma and will gain a narrative of hope, possibility, and healing through connection. *Helping Children with Traumatic Stress*, a companion resource to *The Hero's Mask*, offers accessible evidence-informed tools to support children and families in their journey of healing from trauma. Caregivers,

educators, and therapists will find the curriculum guide with its specific objectives and activities invaluable in supporting connections with children and in providing developmentally-appropriate, culturally-sensitive, trauma-informed care."
Mindy Kronenberg, Ph.D., IMH-E®, Clinical Psychologist and Adjunct Professor, University of Memphis, Co-Editor of *Treating Traumatized Children: A Casebook of Evidence-based Therapies.*

"Brilliant psychoeducation on trauma, resilience and the power of relationships disguised as a middle grade novel. Reading *The Hero's Mask* together should stimulate supportive and healing discussions between middle schoolers and their adult mentors. Overall a wonderful therapeutic resource!"
Laurel J. Kiser, Ph.D., M.B.A., Associate Professor, Division of Psychiatric Services Research, Department of Psychiatry, University of Maryland School of Medicine.

"*The Hero's Mask*, written by a national expert in child traumatic stress, creatively addresses important ways educators, professionals, and caregivers can support a child dealing with pain from trauma and adversity. The *Guidebook* follows along with the novel as Carrie, our middle school role model, engages us with her courage and personality in facing overwhelming feelings, trauma triggers, and broken connections with family and peers that often occur when trauma and grief impact our youth. Kagan's text offer guidance and inspiration to important adults in children's lives to use the power of their relationships in informed, healing, and transformative ways."
Lisa Amaya-Jackson, MD, MPH, Deputy Director, UCLA-Duke National Center for Child Traumatic Stress.

"*The Hero's Mask* books go beyond the growing awareness of ACES and provide practical tools that concerned parents, teachers, counselors and therapists can use to rebuild the emotionally supportive relationships children need to thrive after experiences of hardship and trauma. The novel engages children and caring adults to experience adversity through the eyes of a child including what can help and what can hurt a troubled child. The *Guidebook* provides a curriculum for exploration of heroes that can help children, classrooms and schools to take steps to prevent or

reduce traumatic stress. Together, these books provide essential resources for trauma-informed schools and programs."
Heather Larkin Halloway, Ph.D., Associate Professor, School of Social Welfare, State University of New York at Albany.

"Richard Kagan weaves together story with trauma-informed principles and interventions. As the reader learns about Carrie, her history, her challenges, and her strengths, they are learning important lessons about stress and trauma that they can apply to themselves or those around them. His metaphor of the mask is powerful, and through story, he offers dialogues about heroes, fear and how it affects us, the importance of taking a stand, reaching out for support, and showing up as your authentic self. These dialogues are core to both trauma treatments and trauma-informed systems, and it is refreshing to see them embraced in a story. Children, parents, and teachers will benefit from reading The Hero's Mask, and I strongly believe it will help them open doors to important conversations that lead to healing."
Chandra Ghosh Ippen, Ph.D., Associate Director, Child Trauma Research Program, University of California, San Francisco.

THE HERO'S MASK

The Hero's Mask is an engaging novel about Carrie, an eleven-year old girl and her friends who work together to stop the bullies picking on their classmates as they unravel mysteries in their school. The novel traces Carrie's discovery of strengths within herself, her family and her friends, despite losses and hardships in her family, and how Carrie is inspired by a new teacher who helps her learn the secrets of heroes. *The Hero's Mask* is a story about children and parents/caregivers overcoming fears and healing the wounds separating a mother and daughter, both scarred by traumatic grief.

This book is also available to purchase alongside a guidebook as part of the two-component set, *The Hero's Mask: Helping Children with Traumatic Stress*. This essential resource provides a resiliency-focused guide for promoting trauma-informed schools and child and family services to help children and families experiencing traumatic stress.

Richard Kagan is a clinical psychologist and the author and co-author of 12 books and 35+ articles, chapters, and papers on practice and research issues in trauma therapy, child welfare, foster care, adoption, professional development, program evaluation, and quality improvement in family service and behavioral health care programs. Dr. Kagan's publications highlight practical and innovative approaches that counselors, therapists, educators, parents and caregivers can utilize to help children and families strengthen resilience and reduce traumatic stress.

THE HERO'S MASK

Richard Kagan

Routledge
Taylor & Francis Group

LONDON AND NEW YORK

First published 2021
by Routledge
2 Park Square, Milton Park, Abingdon, Oxon OX14 4RN

and by Routledge
52 Vanderbilt Avenue, New York, NY 10017

Routledge is an imprint of the Taylor & Francis Group, an informa business

British Library Cataloguing-in-Publication Data
A catalogue record for this book is available from the British Library

Library of Congress Cataloging-in-Publication Data
Names: Kagan, Richard, author.
Title: The hero's mask / Richard Kagan.
Description: Abingdon, Oxon ; New York, NY : Routledge, 2021. | Summary: Inspired by a new teacher using stories of heroes to shape the curriculum, eleven-year-old Carrie and her friends work together to stop the bullies picking on their classmates and unravel the mysteries in their school. Includes a note from the author.
Identifiers: LCCN 2020019138 (print) | LCCN 2020019139 (ebook) | ISBN 9780367474317 (pbk) | ISBN 9781003035558 (ebk)
Subjects: CYAC: Heroes--Fiction. | Resilience (Personality trait)--Fiction. | Bullying--Fiction. | Schools--Fiction.
Classification: LCC PZ7.1.K1865 He 2021 (print) | LCC PZ7.1.K1865 (ebook) | DDC [Fic]--dc23
LC record available at https://lccn.loc.gov/2020019138
LC ebook record available at https://lccn.loc.gov/2020019139

ISBN: 978-0-367-47431-7 (pbk)
ISBN: 978-1-003-03555-8 (ebk)

Typeset in Palatino
by MPS Limited, Dehradun

To Laura, my partner in the journey of life,
and
to the next generation of storytellers in my family,
Amit, Gia, Jonah, Maya, Reena, Shayna and Tesi

Contents

For information about how to use *The Hero's Mask* to
promote an understanding of trauma, to help children
and families with traumatic stress and to develop
trauma-informed schools and treatment programs,
please see *Helping Children with Traumatic Stress:
The Hero's Mask Guidebook for Parents, Caregivers,
Educators, Counselors and Therapists.*

Prologue

I took a deep breath as I entered my school gym. Rows and rows of chairs had been set up on the floor. Grown-ups I didn't know were standing around talking. It didn't look the gym I had known for the last six years.

I looked up at the school stage. A large table with 12 chairs had been set up at the front of the left side of the stage for the school board and a smaller table with two chairs was set up on the right side. The men standing near the large table wore dark suits and ties. The women wore dark colored dresses or pantsuits. None of them looked happy to be there.

Up on the stage, Connor, a boy I hated from my fifth-grade class, was shaking hands with the school board president. The school board president smiled at Connor. A large man stood behind Connor with his hand on Connor's shoulder. The man turned his head and stared at the people coming into the gym with hard eyes and pursed lips that seemed to say, 'Don't mess with me or my son.' Suddenly, I felt the man's eyes lock onto mine. Then, I saw Connor and the school board president turn and glare in my direction.

My stomach started to ache. I suddenly felt all alone. All the other kids had mothers and fathers at this meeting. My dad had died a year before and my mom had to work. I didn't know where to go. My legs felt stiff, unable to move. I felt a teardrop grow in my right eye. *What was I doing here? How could I go up on that stage alone?*

I looked back at the gym door. I could run out. *Why did I have to be the one?*

My right leg started stomping the floor, again and again, harder and harder. I took another deep breath and looked down. I knew what my leg was telling me. I had to get up on that stage to save the best teacher I ever had. I had to get up on that stage to save my class from the horrible teacher's aide who would take over when my teacher was gone. I had to get up on that stage because I had failed so badly before.

I shook my head hard to the left. My teardrop flew out into the air. I checked my face: tight lips, tight cheeks, tight eyes. Then, I lifted my head. It was go-time.

This is the story of how I ended up alone in that gym, who tried to stop me from getting on that stage, who helped me, and what happened.

My story starts on a Friday. It was early February, four months before the school board came to my school, three months before the time I almost got arrested, and long before my friends and I solved the mystery that closed down our classroom. It was the Friday when everything started to change.

CHAPTER 1
Tight lips

I woke up before my alarm. Sunshine warmed my room. I bounced out of bed and got dressed in a flash. It was a blue jean day. I put on my favorite dark blue jeans, the ones with holes in the knees that Mom hated, and my bright blue USA Women's Soccer Team t-shirt.

That morning, I felt good, good from my curly blonde hair down to my tingling toes. I didn't know why I felt so good and I *didn't care*. I just found myself humming out loud. It was a happy song, bright and strong. I felt a smile spreading on my lips. I ran downstairs and down the hall into the kitchen. And I *never* did that. In fact, I never did any of those things anymore.

"What are you so happy about?" Mom asked. She looked tired. She sounded tired. Her lips were pressed tightly together and curled downwards into a frown.

"Carrie, you need a sweater and a long sleeve top. It's cold out-side. Did you wash your face? Did you pick up your room? I better *not* find it a mess like yesterday!" Mom looked straight at me and shook her head. Then she turned away from me and went back to preparing breakfast. I froze from my head down to my toes.

I watched the back of Mom's shoulders sag just a little and I could feel Mom's frown growing without even seeing her face. I felt my smile tighten on my face then curve downward into my own deep frown. It felt like some invisible force was pulling my lips down and pushing my cheeks into my chin and my chin into my chest. I could feel Mom's frown growing deeper and deeper into my face.

"Now, run upstairs," Mom said without even turning to look at me. "You're 11 years old. You should know better. Get going!"

I looked down and pinched my lips as I turned around. My birthday was just yesterday and now I had so many more rules to follow. It was so much better to be ten, even better to be five. What *good is* it getting older if all you get is more rules, more stuff you *have* to do. Stuff you *don't want* to do!

"Hurry up," Mom said. "You're going to be late for school."

Mom didn't understand what school was really like. I used to love school but now I hated it. I really thought my teacher, Ms. Craddick, was going to be nice when school started last Fall. She smiled at all of us on the first day and told us this was her first year teaching. Her smile seemed real and she told us she was a little nervous. I liked that.

"I am so excited to be teaching fifth grade at Bartonsville Elementary," Ms. Craddick said on the first day of school. "We're going to set records for excellence this year." Then she started reading directions to us from her teacher's guide-book. She would stop and smile at us as she turned the pages. Boring! Kids started giggling and passing notes. Ms. Craddick clutched the guidebook to her chest. I really wanted her to be a great teacher. I think she really tried but she even had trouble answering questions from kids. Simple stuff. Stuff even I knew.

Things got worse when Ms. Craddick saw our first quiz and test scores. She smiled less, and when she did smile, her smile seemed tight, fake. She kept looking at her teacher's guide as if that would tell her how to lead a fifth-grade class. And when the class didn't respond, she changed. Little lines stretched down her face. I could see her whole body tighten up and start to shake. She tried to act tough. Her voice turned from sweet to shrill. She snapped at kids in the class who were fooling around.

"Stop talking. Listen and learn."

The teacher's aide, Mr. Fricter, made things even worse. Mr. Fricter yelled at students, especially students he didn't like. And the more nervous Ms. Craddick got, the more he yelled.

"Stop talking!" "Get to work!"

Mr. Fricter told the class he had worked for 30 years in a school for juvenile delinquents. He got hurt breaking up a fight between two 14-year-old students in that school and told us he had been recovering from back surgery. I could see his whole face tense up into a frown every time he stood up. With every step, he seemed to shudder just a little and his frown grew deeper. I guess Mom would say he wasn't really yelling at us kids. He was just doing his job and we should have showed respect and listened. But his face looked mean. His voice was harsh and he would point his finger into your face so close you could see the dirt under his fingernails.

"Gross!" I said out loud as I climbed back up the stairs. "School sucks big time. I hate school!"

"Hurry up," Mom called out. "Your oatmeal is getting cold."

I ran the rest of the way up the stairs and threw my blanket over my bed. I tossed the book I was reading on my dresser. Then, I went into the bathroom and splashed some water on my face. It was cold, *brrr!* I looked into the mirror and stared hard at my face. My lips were curled down, just like Mom's. *Yucch!*

"Hurry, Carrie!" Mom yelled up the stairs. "You are going to miss the bus again and I don't have time to drive you to school."

My ears started to burn. I saw a tiny tear grow in my right eye. I shook my head hard to the left and then sharply back to the right. "Not now," I said to myself, shaking away the teardrop. "Not ever. Never ever!" Then, I tensed up my lips until they were pressed hard against each other, straight across, tight and thin. I tightened my cheeks and stared straight into the mirror. My eyes were clear, dry and blue. My lips were pressed hard and firm.

I stared into the mirror and checked my face: tight lips, tight cheeks, tight eyes. I was a 'tough cookie,' as my grandma used to say. But it wasn't really my face. It was my mask and I wouldn't forget it again. My mask worked like a shield. Grown-ups left me alone. Teachers didn't ask me to do anything. Bullies stayed away. My mask kept people from seeing what I was thinking and feeling inside, the things that hurt so bad, the things I didn't want anyone to know.

I threw on an old cable knit sweater, the color of oatmeal. Mom hated this sweater almost as much as she hated my jeans, but it was a gift from Grandma. She knit it special for me so I loved it. And I didn't care what Mom thought.

I stared hard into the mirror. My mouth sagged a little. My face frowned back at me from the mirror. Then I walked down the stairs, quietly this time. My feet moved slowly, step by step, as if lead weights were strapped on each foot and I had to force my legs to move.

"You know, you have other sweaters and jeans without holes," Mom said, hardly looking up from her newspaper. "Now eat fast. Your bus will be here in just a few minutes."

"Brown sugar, please," I asked in my sweetest voice.

"Sorry, honey, we ran out." Mom shook her head slowly. She looked down at the table and her shoulders seemed to drop another notch. I thought I saw a tear in her right eye but Mom quickly lifted her head. Then, she went back to reading the newspaper.

I could see the top headline, *Auto Plant Closes; 900 Jobs Lost*. Mom took a deep breath and sighed. I watched her frown grow deeper and deeper. I felt my own lips curl down. I shuddered. I felt my legs kicking wildly under the table. I never wanted to look like that. Never ever!

"I want a banana," Kevin said in his sweet, little voice. Kevin was four years old. He had light brown hair, sparkling big, blue eyes, and chunky cheeks. Kevin spoke in a chirpy voice that sounded like bells ringing. He was so cute it was hard to resist picking him up and hugging him tight. But recently, even Kevin had become a pain to me.

Kevin was always coming into my room, taking my stuff, my good stuff. I kept finding my most special things broken when I came home from school. And I didn't want to hear Kevin's chirpy voice asking me to play with him. So, I screamed, "Get out. Leave me alone!" as loud as I could whenever he came into my room. Then, I'd turn my head away. I didn't want to see the sad look on his face. My stomach already hurt almost all the time. Seeing Kevin's sad face just made my stomach hurt even more.

"You can have the last banana," Mom said softly, slicing the banana carefully for Kevin, just the way he liked it. Mom spread the banana slices on his cereal and gently rubbed Kevin's back.

I looked at Kevin but didn't say a word. This sucked too. How come Kevin got what he wanted and all I got was plain old oatmeal! Worse, my oatmeal had turned cold and dried out, hard as cement. *Yuchh.*

"Bus will be here in eight minutes," Mom said as she sat back down and turned to the next page of the newspaper.

I heaped a big spoonful of sugar on my oatmeal while Mom was reading. I quickly ate my oatmeal, then got up and gulped down a glass of milk. Mom looked up at the clock. I grabbed my coat and ran out the door.

"Out of here," I said and slammed the door behind me.

I stood for a second on the front steps. Snow melted into the grass around me releasing a faint scent of moist earth and new life. My dad used to say that you could smell springtime coming if you tried really hard. I took a deep breath of fresh air and gazed up at wispy white clouds that melted into a bright blue sky.

For just a moment, I closed my eyes. I tasted the damp air in my mouth. It was February but I imagined flowers blooming. I remembered how I used to love running outside with Mom and Dad and Kevin on spring days.

I tried not to think of missing Dad but a teardrop grew again in my right eye. Another teardrop followed and I could feel another one coming. My stomach started hurting. I felt all mixed up inside, hurt and angry and sad. I had gone from humming and skipping to tears in less than 20 minutes. And now, I was mad. *I would not be like Mom. I would never give up. I would never let myself cry again. Never ever!* I turned my head sharply to the left and sent my tears flying into the wind.

I threw my backpack over my shoulder. A cold breeze stung my face as I stepped away from the house. I pressed my lips tighter and headed into the winter wind.

CHAPTER 2
Tick tock tick tock tick

I ran to the corner just as my school bus was pulling up. I gulped one last breath of cold fresh air as the bus door opened. Then, I climbed up the steps, two at a time. I've got long legs and I use them. I plopped myself down on the first empty seat I saw and gazed out the window at my house as the bus slowly pulled away. My house looked the same as always, but I knew it wasn't. It never would be.

I heard voices I recognized. I looked around the bus. Two boys had their heads bent down, whispering to each other. I knew them, Chad and Connor, fifth graders from my class. I could tell right off they were up to no good. Over the last five months, those two had gotten away with sneaky stuff, like taking things from other kids' desks or poking kids in the back. Then when the boy or girl who got poked cried out, Mr. Fricter would yell at that kid, like it was their fault.

And if one of the kids complained, Chad and Connor acted like they were the sweetest little angels in the whole wide world. Connor opened up his big blue eyes and began to pout as he looked up at the teacher. Teachers loved that look. Blond hair, chunky cheeks, clothes that seemed a size too big. They felt sorry for him.

"Poor Connor, such a nice boy to teachers. So helpful," teachers said. And Chad would put on his sad, lost little boy look. Teachers loved that one too. I heard one teacher tell another that Chad had been placed into some kind of group home for abused children when he was younger. That's where he and Connor became friends.

"Poor Chad. He just needs a little help," teachers said.

I felt sad for whatever happened to Chad and Connor but they shouldn't have been allowed to take it out on other kids. That was just wrong! I had seen Connor use his 'sweet angel' look and Chad use his fake pout since second grade. Some teachers seemed to know they were faking it but Ms. Craddick and Mr. Fricter never caught on. They'd scowl at the kids who complained about Chad and Connor and tell them to get back to work. And they would nod their heads with deep concern when Chad and Connor talked about how other kids were mean to them. Ms. Craddick and Mr. Fricter gave them special jobs, like going to the gym to get playground balls for recess while the rest of us had to sit in class.

It wasn't fair. My legs started jerking back and forth, back and forth, back and forth. I was stuck in my seat but my legs were jerking as if they were trying somehow to kick Chad or Connor. They deserved it!

I looked around the bus again. Most of the kids sat quietly, holding their backpacks on their laps. No one was smiling. Hardly anyone was talking. Some kids had a glassy look in their eyes like they were a million miles away.

It wasn't always this way. I remembered how I used to be happy to get on the bus. I used to smile at my friends and even at the school bus driver. Kids smiled back and laughed. That was before the 'hard times' in our town. Before so many people lost their jobs. Before everything got so bad.

I missed Mr. Cook. He used to be my bus driver. Mr. Cook would greet each of the kids with a big smile and a twinkle in his eye. He had white hair and wrinkles on his dark brown face that seemed to stretch as he smiled.

"How y'all doing today?" he'd ask. "Hop on board Carrie!" And, some days, I would do just that. I'd hop on the bus like a bunny rabbit.

"What ya' cookin' today?" I'd ask Mr. Cook, smiling back at him. "I know it's going to be yummy."

"Lunch is going to be a SUPER SPECIAL SURPRISE," he'd say with a big grin.

It was more than a joke. Mr. Cook also worked in the cafeteria and I still saw him once in a while helping to prepare lunch. Before this last year, he had also helped serve food to the kids. Mr. Cook used to know all the kids' names from his bus. He gave them a big smile when they got their meal. Mr. Cook made a regular old school lunch seem super special.

The new driver just stared at the road. She hardly even looked at the kids. She just looked at us through her mirrors as if it was too hard to turn her head around. I wondered if she'd rather see us all in a mirror than see us 'for real.'

The new bus driver's face seemed flat like she had no feelings at all. Maybe, she didn't care. Or, maybe she was too tired. Maybe, she worked a second or a third job. That's what my mother did now.

"Just to get by," Mom said, nodding her head. "Just to get by.... Just for a little while," she would say again a little louder, as if she had to convince herself this was really true. I didn't believe it. Not for a second.

I stared at the bus driver. Maybe the new bus driver was wearing a mask, just like I did. Just like the other kids on the bus with their blank looks. A 'school driver mask.' Silent lips, dull eyes, flat face. Not showing what she felt. Not saying what she thought. Not saying anything that really meant anything. Not really being there. Fake. Fake. Fake.

That was the new way people acted in town. It was like the Mayor had decreed a new law for how people should act. 'Don't say nothin' to nobody.' I didn't even know the bus driver's name. And no way was I going to ask.

I reached deep inside my backpack, feeling for the hidden pocket. I pulled out a crumpled photo. In the photo, my dad was cradling me in my arms, a proud smile on his face. My mom was gazing up

9

at my dad and me. She was smiling. Her eyes were sparkling, laughing. In the distance, gentle waves rolled onto a sandy beach. I remembered how the sun warmed my face and the smell of the ocean air. I felt my legs slow down and stop kicking but my lips started to quiver. A teardrop began to swell in my right eye again. I tried to blink it away and slid the photo back inside my backpack. I would not cry.

Just then, the bus stopped. Cami got on. Cami's real name was Camille, but no one called her that. She was my best friend, and had been, back to first grade. We had shared everything since then, clothes, birthdays, even secrets.

"Hey," Cami said with a smile as she sat down next to me.

"Back at you!" I said. We did our secret fist bump. We tapped three sides of our fists together, right side, left side, and then our knuckles. It was a three-sided fist-bump. Then, we whispered, "We are the best!" Cami and I used to sing out, "We are the best!" loud and strong with a laugh and a smile, but now we said it with a whisper. No sense getting the bus driver angry.

"Ready for school?" Cami pressed her lips together and imitated Ms. Craddick's shrill voice and fake smile. "Okay, Class 5D, Listen to me. No time to play. It's work all day!" Cami opened her eyes wide. "Yes, kids, tick, tock, tick, tock, tick. IT'S TIME FOR A-RITH-ME-TIC!"

"Woo hoo!" I said and then switched to the voice Ms. Craddick used when she read to us from her teacher's guide. "Blah, blah, blah, blah, reading. Blah, blah, blah, blah, writing." Then I bent over, clutched my belly and moaned, "Blah, blah, blah, Ms. Craddick. YOU ARE MA-KING ME SICK!" I pretended to puke all over the bus seat. I could see the corners of Cami's mouth light up with a smile.

"And Mr. Stricter will march around the room yelling 'Ick, ick, icker. I'll make you even sicker!'" Cami said laughing.

The new bus driver turned and glared at both of us. The bus had stopped. I noticed how the bus driver's nose seemed to widen.

The driver squinted her eyes, making them look smaller which gave her large, round face a very angry look. It was also a very funny look, if you looked at it just the right way. It was another mask. I was sure of it now.

I felt my own mask snap back in place on my face—tight lips, tight cheeks, tight eyes. I was ready for school.

All the kids grabbed their backpacks and ran off the bus with Chad and Connor leading the way. Both of the boys wore nasty looks on their faces. Not quite smiles, more like mean grins. Looks like trouble today, I thought.

Just then, Cami grabbed my arm.

"I've got a new CD to show you. Got it from my aunt yesterday."

One of the things I liked about Cami was that she didn't care if she didn't have the latest tech or apps. She was happy to put a cd into an old cd player when other kids were bringing the latest smart phones or tablets to school and bragged about how they had downloaded some 'hot' free music with the latest streaming app. Cami just seemed happy to play great music and didn't care what she used to play it. I liked that.

"Come over to my house after school," Cami said excitedly.

"Super cool!" I said. 'Super cool' was something my grandma used to say. I grabbed Cami's hand and we ran into the school building.

CHAPTER 3
'Listen and learn'

I was busy working on math when Ms. Craddick suddenly stood up from her desk. She began pacing back and forth in front of the room. Her head was bent down. Her body was shaking. Ms. Craddick seemed to be staring at the floor but her eyes looked glazed. I wondered if she was really seeing anything at all.

My stomach started to hurt a little. It was a little burn, like a small alarm going off in my gut. Then my legs started kicking faster and faster. I looked around. None of the other kids seemed to notice. But I knew something was about to happen.

Ms. Craddick suddenly spun around and faced the class.

"Class 5D students." Ms. Craddick paused. She always called us 'Class 5D students,' as if we didn't know our classroom was Room D in the fifth-grade wing of our school. And she said the 'D,' in a way that made it sound like the whole class was barely above an 'F.' Every student was just about to fail. And she, Ms. Craddick, had the so-very-difficult job of trying to teach such a terrible group of kids.

"I have something to tell you," Ms. Craddick said. "My husband found a new job." Ms. Craddick's chin dropped to the floor for a second. Then she jerked her head back and she stared at the class with blank eyes. I wondered if she was even seeing us at all. Ms. Craddick took a deep breath and stared straight ahead as if she was talking to the back wall. "It's in another city. My husband and I have to move quickly."

Ms. Craddick stared down at the floor again as though something was down there. I saw teardrops start to form in Ms. Craddick's

eyes. Ms. Craddick took a sharp breath and sighed. Her eyes seemed to glisten. I started to feel sorry for her. Maybe she was not so bad. I never even knew she was married. Maybe she was going through hard times too. Maybe that's why she was so nervous.

Ms. Craddick looked up and tightened her lips. Her whole face changed. The teardrops were gone and she glared at all of us. I could see little lines extending down into tight cheeks and a pursed mouth that seemed to warn everyone in capital letters, "DON'T PUSH ME!" It was another mask, Ms. Craddick's mask.

Ms. Craddick looked left and right again, her eyes sweeping across the classroom, daring any girl or boy to meet her eyes, or worse, to say anything, even to raise their hand to ask a question. Those were Ms. Craddick's rules for the class since we started doing so poorly on class tests: 'Listen to what I say. Don't interrupt. Do your work. Don't talk.'

Ms. Craddick's lips began to move again.

"Today, you will finish the next two chapters of your math book. That means, you will do the assignments at the end of the chapter and the worksheets Mr. Fricter will pass out. Read the worksheets and put your answers on your own paper. There should be ten pages of work to do. And you will write a ten-page report on snakes, neatly, for science, building on what we read yesterday. Now, get out your math book. Turn to Chapter 18. Read it then do the assignment at the end of the chapter."

Crystal groaned softly. I liked Crystal. I also knew that Crystal was afraid of snakes. She hated them. In third grade, our teacher had kept a pet garter snake in a cage. I really liked our third-grade teacher. I even touched the snake once when our teacher held its head. But Crystal wouldn't go near that side of the classroom for the whole school year. Every time the snake cage was opened, her lips trembled, her eyes went blank, her mouth opened wide, and her whole body seemed to freeze.

"Something wrong?" Ms. Craddick asked. Ms. Craddick was staring now at Crystal. Her voice was sharp. It didn't sound like a

question. The whole class was silent, like we were waiting for something, something bad to happen. Ms. Craddick pursed her lips. "Get to work or *you* will write a 20-page report on snakes. Poisonous snakes."

I could see Crystal shrink back into her seat. Ms. Craddick began scanning the faces of the other students again. She shook her head and pursed her lips. Then, she took in another deep breath and looked straight ahead as if she was talking again to the back wall of the classroom.

"You will have a new teacher Monday. Her name is Ms. Kramer. And she will expect your work to be done on time and done right, the way I taught you."

Ms. Craddick's eyes swept left and right, over the class. I could see that everyone was sitting stiffly, like stick dolls, staring straight ahead. No one dared to talk or even to move. More masks, I thought, masks that stretched over our whole bodies from our heads to our toes.

"In case of any problems, Mr. Fricter will be here." The left side of Ms. Craddick's lips rose higher than the right side with every word, like she was half-smiling and half-frowning. "He will check and make sure you do your work. He will also finish class today." With that, she turned away from the class and sat down at her desk.

Mr. Fricter stood up and for just a second, I saw him wince like he had been hurt. Then, his face tightened into his usual frown. Mr. Fricter started walking up and down the rows. He stopped by Crystal's desk and stared at her work for a long time. Then, he growled and moved on to the next unlucky student.

I couldn't wait to get out of school and talk to Cami. Every minute seemed like an hour that day. I kept looking up at the clock. I had so much to say to Cami that I could hardly do any math.

One time, when I looked up, Mr. Fricter was standing right in front of the clock. Mr. Fricter was tall with broad shoulders, light brown

hair, and a pale face that gave him a ghost-like look. Mr. Fricter stared back at me from across the classroom, as if he knew what I was thinking. Like he knew I wanted to get out of his class so badly and he hated me for even daring to look up at him, for even daring to want to escape. He kept staring at me. I stared back. For a second, I wondered if he was daring me to say something, anything. I knew that was crazy. I quickly looked down at my math work sheet.

I did a couple more math problems then looked up another time. This time I saw Chad walking slowly up to Mr. Fricter. Ms. Craddick had left the room.

"Could you help me, please?" Chad asked in his soft, 'poor me' voice with a little frown on his face. He looked small and needy.

Another mask. I could tell it was fake a mile away. But not Mr. Fricter. He smiled, a little toothy smile. Then, he started looking over Chad's worksheet, like Chad really wanted to learn something and Mr. Fricter was the greatest teacher in the world. *What a sucker!*

Then, out of the corner of my eye, I saw Connor leaning over to the side of his desk. His arm was stretched out toward Crystal's desk. Crystal was in the back row and sat next to Chad and Connor. All the other students sat in front of them.

Crystal and all the other students were watching Chad do his 'poor me' show. In a flash, I saw Connor's arm reach over and grab Crystal's math papers, all the work she had done that afternoon. It only took a second and his hand was gone. Connor pretended he was hard at work at his desk.

"Hey!" Crystal screamed.

Mr. Fricter looked up, his lips curled downward into a sneer. "Something the matter with *you* again?" Mr. Fricter's voice was like a growl, deep, hoarse, and mean. He winced again standing up then stomped to the back of the room and glared down at Crystal. "Where's your math homework?"

Crystal froze like she was about to be hit by a truck. All her work was gone. Her lips started trembling. She seemed to be trying say something. Just then, the bell rang.

"Everyone *sit down* until I tell you, *you* can leave," Mr. Fricter looked slowly around the room. "Okay. Everyone can go. Except *you*," he said, glaring at Crystal. The left edge of his mouth curled up just a little. "You need to answer at least three pages of math problems before you can leave. I believe that's about 60 problems. We don't just sit around in this classroom, young lady."

"But ..." Crystal said.

"Listen and learn," Mr. Fricter ordered. He pointed his index finger at Crystal's face and clenched the rest of his fingers and thumb into a fist. "Listen and learn," he repeated slowly, biting out each word. With that, he turned away.

Crystal was shaking now. I wanted to do something, but what could I do? I wanted to say something, but to who? *Who really cared?*

Ms. Craddick was out of the classroom and she wouldn't do anything anyway. She never had all year. Chad and Connor had gotten away with all kinds of stuff for the last five months. I felt bad. I had done nothing all year but watch those two boys get away with their dirty tricks, even when kids I liked got hurt. I felt my forehead squeeze tight. My heart pumped harder and faster. I tried to think of something I could do. My legs started jerking back and forth.

Mr. Fricter was watching the students as they grabbed their backpacks. They walked as fast as they could to the door, trying to get out of the classroom quickly before Mr. Fricter kept them behind like Crystal.

I saw Connor already at the door with Chad right behind him snickering. Connor had probably hidden Crystal's papers in his bag or coat. Later, he and Chad would copy Crystal's work. Everyone in the class knew that Crystal was an 'A' student. There would be no proof of Chad and Connor stealing and cheating. It wasn't fair. I had to do something.

I knew that Mr. Fricter would never believe me if I told him. Ms. Craddick and Mr. Fricter had called me a troublemaker from the first week of class. I had never had teachers who were so angry at me. They had already given me six detentions this year for what they called 'disrupting the class.' As the weeks and months went by, I started to wonder if it was true. Maybe I was a troublemaker.

In the first weeks of fifth grade, I had done what I always had done. I raised my hand and asked questions about what was going on, about things Ms. Craddick said that didn't make any sense. Only Ms. Craddick didn't like questions. I could see her start to shake a little. Sometimes she would re-read something from her teacher's manual. I know she tried to help but what she said didn't make any sense.

"This is stupid," I mumbled.

"What did you say?" Ms. Craddick asked. That led to my first detention. The next two were for talking during class. I got three more for kicking at my desk.

The next time I asked a question, Ms. Craddick said, "You need to pay attention. Next time, *listen* a little better." And the third time I asked a question, Ms. Craddick got out of her chair, marched over to my desk and stared long and hard, looking down at me. She opened my notebook and saw how I had been drawing pages and pages of angry faces, scared faces, and sad faces along with cars and trucks crashing into each other. Then, she asked me, "Did you see the new school banner in the school lobby when you came in today?"

"Yes," I said in a tiny voice that I didn't even recognize was my own. I felt my heart tremble. My stomach ached. Ms. Craddick's voice cut like a knife. Each word she said seemed to cut through my belly and tear at my gut.

"And what did it say?"

"Listen and learn to achieve." My voice was faint like I had no air left in my lungs to speak out.

"That means, teachers talk. Students listen. My job is to teach. Your job is to listen. Don't draw pictures when you should be listening. Don't ask me questions when *you* should be doing *your* work. *Listen* and *learn* what I teach." Then, Ms. Craddick turned away.

After that, no one in the class asked any questions, not a single one for days and days. It was the quietest classroom I had ever known. It was like the whole class had lost their voices. It was like no one was really there.

"Something wrong with *you* today? Do you need some extra help, like your friend?" Mr. Fricter asked, waking me up from my thoughts.

I looked up and saw him standing by my desk, glaring down at me. All the other kids had left the classroom, except Crystal and me. I shook my head and said very softly, "No, sir." Then, I gathered up my math papers as Mr. Fricter turned away.

I folded my worksheets and put them in my science book. I also crumpled some spare paper in my left hand. Then, I grabbed my other books, stuffed them in my backpack and stood up. I held my science book in my right hand. But, instead of walking to the door, I walked to the back of the classroom holding the crumpled papers. I pretended I was going to toss them in the garbage can in the back of the room.

Out of the corner of my eye, I saw Mr. Fricter walk to the door of the classroom. He was watching kids in my class head down the hall to their buses. Mr. Fricter placed his hand on the door's edge, like he was getting ready to shut it at any moment, locking in the unlucky children left behind.

I quietly placed my science book on Crystal's desk as I walked by.

"Look at page 31," I said. "Copy my papers. Then meet me at Cami's house." I didn't even look back. I just kept on walking to the back of the room. I dropped the crumpled papers in the garbage can, turned, and headed for the door.

CHAPTER 4
The three Cs

I spotted Cami standing by the school entrance and quickly grabbed her hand. Chad and Connor were standing by the bus, snickering and whispering to another boy.

"Let's get out of here. I've got to tell you something. Forget the bus," I said. We took off, running down the street towards Cami's house.

Cami lived just a few blocks away from me. I liked Cami's parents and wished I had a younger sister like Cami did. Cami's sister was so cute and always seemed to be helping instead of getting in the way like Kevin was doing these days. Cami's mother cooked super delicious food every time I came over like 'Chana Masala,' 'Roti' and 'Dal.' Just saying some of the names made me feel hungry.

Cami's mother was from India and Cami's father was from Canada.

"Quebec," he said proudly. Cami's father taught chemistry and physics at the high school. Her mother was a computer programmer. Sometimes, Cami's mother talked in Hindi and her father talked in French.

"Ahh, Carrie," Cami's father would say with a smile. "Parlez-vous français aujourd'hui?"

"Oui. Oui," I always said. Those were the only French words I knew. Cami could speak French and Hindi. That was so awesome!

Cami's mother greeted us at the door with big hugs, even though she didn't know I was coming.

"Come in and have something to eat," she said with a smile. Cami's mother always gave us snacks after school. I could smell something simmering on the oven cooktop.

"We're having palak paneer, chana masala, and roti for dinner tonight. Would you like to stay for dinner?"

My eyes lit up.

"Yes, she can," said Cami, not even waiting for me to answer. "And sleep over tonight too! It's Friday. No school tomorrow! You can listen to my new cd. We'll watch a couple movies ..."

"And what about your homework?" Cami's mother asked.

"I've got all weekend. Pl-e-a-s-e, can Carrie stay?"

"That means you've got to start on homework first thing Sunday and *nothing else* until you're done," Cami's mother said. Cami nodded. "And Carrie has to get her mother's permission."

"Thanks," I said, and in a flash, I called Mom at her job and worked it all out. Mom said she would drop off some clothes and my toothbrush later that night.

Cami and I gobbled up toasted waffles with peanut butter, applesauce, and red grapes. I looked up at Cami. With a nod and quick "thanks" to Cami's mother, we grabbed our backpacks and headed to Cami's room.

"Yea!!! No more Ms. Craddick," Cami said, quickly closing the door.

"Wait! I've got something bigger," I said. "Did you see what Chad and Connor did?" I couldn't wait for an answer. "They stole Crystal's math homework and got her in trouble with Mr. Fricter. That's why she's stuck at school right now." I took a deep breath. "But not for long." I felt my eyes brighten.

"What happened?" Cami asked.

Just then, we heard voices outside and someone knocking on the door.

"You've got another friend at the door," Cami's mother said. It was Crystal. Cami's mother insisted that she have something to eat, and a few minutes later, we were back in Cami's room.

"You should have seen Mr. Fricter's eyes when I showed him my math papers. He couldn't believe it. I thought his eyes were going to pop out of his head," Crystal said laughing, her head nodding up and down. Crystal always did that when she was excited. She talked real fast, like the words were tumbling out of her head.

Crystal imitated Mr. Fricter, in a pretend deep voice, with a fake frown and narrowed eyes. "Pretty fast work. These better be good. I hope you learned a lesson today."

"Oh, I did," Crystal said using her hyper sweet voice. "I *sure* did, Mr. Fricter. I've learned *so very much* in your class!"

"Super cool!" I said.

"I even made it out in time to catch the bus," Crystal said. "The bus driver was so busy yelling at a couple kids that she left late."

"What's going on?" Cami asked. "Tell me!"

"Okay. Here's what happened," I said. "Chad and Connor were up to their nasty stuff again. I saw Chad faking Mr. Fricter out with his 'poor me' routine. Then, Connor swiped Crystal's math work. Crystal complained and Mr. Fricter got mad at Crystal."

"After the bell, Carrie snuck me her math answers," Crystal said. "You saved me having to stay there alone with Mr. Fricter. I thought I was going to die!"

"He's a whack job!" I said, stomping my foot.

"But what's going to happen now?" Crystal asked. "Ms. Craddick is leaving. We could be left with Mr. Fricter."

"He's worse than she is," Cami said.

Crystal shuddered. "He's nasty, creepy. I hate the way he looks at me."

"And why couldn't Craddick even stay to say goodbye?" Cami asked. "She couldn't even look at us at the end of the day."

"Whatever ..." Crystal said, shaking her head. "I'm glad she's gone! Stupidest teacher, I ever had. I watched her every day trying to figure out what to do, like she was just learning the math or whatever else she was supposed to teach us. She'd be reading the lesson book while she made us work. And she didn't know what she was talking about half the time. All she knew how to do was give us assignments."

"Something else is going on with Ms. Craddick," I said. "It doesn't make sense. It's like she's been playing us."

"She was," Cami said. Then she lowered her voice. "If she was really married, why didn't she ever tell us? How come she didn't wear a ring?"

"Why can't teachers tell us what's really going on?" I asked. "Why do they always hide things? Why can't they tell us the truth?"

"They say it's because we can't handle what's really going on," Cami said. "But really, it's them. They just don't want us asking nosy questions about stuff they don't want to talk about. They *can't* deal with what's really happening."

"Well, *we* can!" Crystal said.

"Let's make a pledge," I said, looking at my friends, "never to be fakes to each other. Never ever!"

"And to stand up for each other when anyone of us is in trouble," Cami said.

"We'll be *The Three Cs!*" Crystal said.

"*The Three Cs* should mean something, more than our names," I said. I can get real serious when something is important.

"Courageous," Cami said smiling.

"Clever and cool," Crystal said.

"*Courageous*, because we dare to learn the truth," I said.

"Clever, because we figure out what's really going on," Cami said.

"And Cool, because we're tight with each other," Crystal said smiling. "We're cool. Nobody's fool."

Cami and I taught Crystal how to do our secret fist bump, tapping three sides of our fists together, right side, left side, and then our knuckles. Then, I took each of their hands and made them into fists placing one fist from Cami on top of one fist from Crystal with one of my fists on top of Crystal's fist. Then, we repeated this with our other fists so we had six fists, white, brown, and black stacked together. It was a fist-bump power-tower.

"Friends forever, stick together," I said.

Crystal and Cami nodded. Then, Cami, Crystal and I said it again together, so loud people in the whole building could hear us. "Friends forever, stick together."

"What's going on in there?" Cami's mother asked from the kitchen. We giggled.

"And one more thing," Cami said. "Each time we win, we celebrate."

"Cool and classy," Crystal said.

Cami opened the door and we headed for the kitchen. Palak paneer, dal and chana simmered on the cooktop tantalizing our noses.

CHAPTER 5
C code

Cami's mother invited Crystal to stay for dinner and after a quick phone call, Crystal was set to stay for dinner and a sleepover.

Cami's father came home and looked at Cami, then Crystal, then me, and back to Cami. He could see the sparkles in our eyes.

"What's up?" he asked.

Cami and Crystal smiled back at him.

"I know something's going on," he said. Then, he grinned and looked hard into Cami's eyes. "Cami?"

"Oh, just an other day, mon cher père," Cami said. "Nothing special. Just the us-u-al stuff."

Crystal giggled.

"Right ..." Cami's mother said. "Out with it!"

Cami looked at Crystal who shrugged her shoulders. I nodded.

"Okay. Well, Ms. Craddick is leaving." Cami said. "We're getting a new teacher Monday."

Cami's father frowned. "School policy is to notify parents ahead of any teacher leaving. Unless it's some kind of emergency ..."

"That's what I thought," I said.

"Is Ms. Craddick sick?" Cami's mother asked.

"She didn't look sick," Crystal said. "She said she had to move because her husband got a new job."

"Something is going on," I said.

"And we're going to find out," Cami said.

Cami's mother and father looked back and forth at each of us, but mostly at Cami.

"Don't worry," Cami said. Then she looked at her mother. "Anyway, how was work today, Amma, Papa?"

"We were talking about school," Cami's mother said sternly, but her face stayed soft and she didn't look angry. "School work has got to come first. No matter what mysteries are going on with your teacher. That's for the school to deal with."

"And then your piano lessons and practice, *before* detective work," Cami's father said, but there was a bright look in his eyes.

"We'll make sure Cami does her schoolwork and practices piano," I said.

Later that night, Cami pulled out the CD her aunt had given her. It was an old CD by a trio of country singers. Before making this CD, the lead singer had criticized an American president and then some people started saying the singers were traitors. The first song Cami played was about how the singers refused to stop speaking their minds, even when someone threatened that they better shut up and sing or their lives would be ended. I thought of Chad and Connor and other kids like them that I had known at school. Instead of giving into people who threatened to kill or hurt them, the singers wrote this song. They began singing all over the world about standing up to people who make threats.

I wanted to be like them, so smart, so strong, so confident they could go on singing on stage in front of a thousand people. They didn't get stuck feeling hurt or scared or mad all the time, like

25

I did. Instead, they somehow put all their feelings into fighting for what they believed in.

"This can be our song, *The Three Cs'* song," I said. Cami and Crystal agreed.

"We need a signal," Crystal said, "a way we can let each other know, when something is going on, like when someone is in trouble."

"Four taps," I said. "Like this: Long, Short, Long, Short." My dad taught me that's the letter C. It's Morse code. We can repeat it three times for *The Three Cs*." I shuddered inside thinking about Dad but I didn't let my friends see it.

"Or, if you can't make a sound, just tap your left ear," Cami said, tapping her ear—Long, Short, Long, Short.

That night, we watched two movies on-line before we went to sleep. One movie was from India and showed people breaking into dancing and singing every few minutes. I wondered why people in our town didn't dance or sing or even smile much anymore. Everyone seemed so serious these days, so down. It was like something had been taken away.

The other movie was from the Harry Potter series. Harry was brave enough to do what most of the adults couldn't do, like saying out loud the name of the evil wizard that the other wizards, even the teachers, were scared of. But Harry had his own problems and he made mistakes. And he had to go to school to learn how to use magical skills, instead of just knowing them somehow. He had to read books, go to classes, practice, and pass tests, just like us.

Bad things had happened to Harry, the worst. Harry got into trouble and he doubted himself. I kept thinking about one scene in the movie where Harry had said something close to what I sometimes wondered. Something I had never shared, not even with Cami. Harry told his godfather that he felt angry all the time and feared that he was becoming mean or bad. That's what I wondered about myself, especially these last few months. Mom always seemed so mad at me. Ms. Craddick and Mr. Fricter hated me. The new bus driver glared at me. And our gym teacher yelled at me last week in front of all the other kids.

I didn't mean to get in trouble but I had grown-ups telling me I broke some stupid rules. Teachers looked at me like I did something horrible, like I was bad. And, then, I'd feel like doing something bad, very bad.

In the movie, Harry's godfather had told Harry that he was not mean or bad but rather a good person who had experienced terrible things. I thought about that. It was becoming harder and harder to remember the good times in my life. But the bad times were strong and kept playing over and over like movies in my mind. Some of the movies were so bad I wouldn't let myself remember them. Other movies were loud and clear with bright colors that wouldn't fade. Like the night Dad said his law firm lost three of their biggest contracts and he and his partners had to break up the business. Dad said he'd have to look for another place to work and maybe work for a law firm out of town. His brother, my Uncle Phil, worked for a big law firm in a large city. He offered Dad a job. Dad had looked so down. His shoulders were slumped and he walked like an old man, bent over like his head was going to sink into the floor. I had never seen Dad look like that.

Then there were the arguments Mom and Dad started having, usually about money. I could see their faces so clearly in my mind it hurt my head just remembering. I tried to push these memories away but it felt like I couldn't escape the bad times. It was like my parents were arguing somehow right in front of me every time I remembered what happened. Their voices, loud, sharp, and raw, reverberated in my ears. I couldn't shut them out or turn the sound down. And the pictures in my mind were worse. I could see Mom's lips pursed with her 'mad as hell' look, the one that made me shiver inside, up and down. And Dad's eyes looked so hard, so cold, when he was mad at Mom. He looked so different than the dad I loved, the fun dad who used to do things with me. His cheeks became so tight that I could almost feel his jaws clench.

I remembered every word Mom and Dad said in their fights, especially the mean ones. In my mind, I could see the words flying between them like little daggers, tiny but sharp. Some of the daggers hit the walls with a crashing sound. Sometimes, I imagined daggers piercing my parents' skin and blood trickling out of their wounds. And after that came more yelling, more little daggers. It was like a nightmare that never ended.

My Dad's law firm broke up and he started working out of town with my uncle a couple days a week, then all week, every week. Mom started working longer hours at her job. Both of them seemed tired all the time and acted snippy towards each other. On weekends, they often didn't look at each other, or, even say 'hello.' They acted like two strangers sharing the same house, the same children, and hating that they had to share. It was so wrong! My stomach started to burn, just thinking about Mom and Dad.

"Time to get up," a soft voice said. I felt someone gently tapping my shoulder. "Wake up sleepyhead! You've been thrashing in your bed, moaning 'Stop', 'Come back',

'Stop,' 'Come back.'" I opened my eyes just enough to see Cami by my side but I didn't move. My mind was overloaded with memories of the bad times that never seemed to go away.

"Get up sleepy head," Cami said, a little louder now. "Crystal had to go home but we saved some breakfast for you. There's pancakes, blueberry pancakes, really sweet ..."

I sat up and sleepily followed Cami into the kitchen. Cami's mother greeted me with a warm hug and the sweet smell of hot maple syrup and pancakes. I piled a stack of pancakes on my plate and covered them with syrup. It was real maple syrup, not the fake kind. Blueberries melted in my mouth.

I remembered Dad making pancakes on Saturday mornings.

"Mo' cake pweeze," Kevin would say.

Then, I would say, "Yummy for the tummy." Kevin would smile at me.

"Yummies for two tummies, coming up," Dad would call out and bring us more pancakes and hot maple syrup. I felt a warm feeling grow in my belly but I caught myself just before I started to smile. I pushed the memory away. One memory led to another. That was too much. *Better to just forget.*

CHAPTER 6

A new friend

After breakfast, I walked home. Along the way, I couldn't help thinking again about Mom and Dad, how they had argued so much after Dad had his job problems. Dad had started living weekdays with Uncle Phil. At first, he called home every night, but then he started missing nights. Then, he started telling us he had to work weekends on his 'big cases.'

"See you soon," he'd say.

"Get real," I had wanted to tell him. But I didn't say anything. Maybe I should have. Maybe that's what I did wrong.

I missed playing games with Dad. We used to make up songs, silly songs, but it was fun. Dad even made up a special bedtime song for me when I was little, putting his own words to the music of an old folk song. I remembered it was always about how I was growing and doing wonderful things, year by year. The song always began "Oh, once I had a little girl. She was so very small. And then that girl began to grow. She became so tall ..." I couldn't remember anything else anymore. Worse, I couldn't remember the last time I had heard Dad sing. It was before he lost his job. Before everything got so hard.

Mom had changed too. She spent more and more time in her bedroom when she wasn't working. Mom used to call me, 'honey' or 'sweetie.' But in the last two years, she hardly even seemed to notice me. And when she did come out of her room and talk to me, it was mostly to tell me all the things I had done wrong. Or, she gave me new chores to do around the house.

The week before, I had a stomach flu and Mom hardly seemed to notice. I remembered how Mom used to get me ginger ale and lemon Italian Ice. And she made me chicken soup when I was sick. She would sit on my bed and gently massage my back, up and down my spine and over my shoulders. Mom's hands felt soft and warm. It felt like she was gently squeezing all the pain out of my body. Then, she rubbed in good feelings, round and round, warm and strong. Mom would wrap her arms around me and hug me tight. After that, she would read me my favorite stories. At bedtime, Mom would tuck me in and sing lullabies, 'Hush, little baby, don't you cry,' or 'Puff the magic dragon.' They were little kid's songs. But I still loved them when Mom sang to me.

Now, I wondered if Mom even knew when I was sick. My stomach started to ache as I stepped on to the gravel driveway leading to our house. I didn't even remember walking down my own street.

"Hey," someone said.

I looked up and saw a boy about my height standing in our neighbor's front yard. I had walked right by him, so lost in my memories that I hadn't even seen him.

"Do you just walk by people and not even say anything?" the boy asked. "That, the way things work in this town?" The boy was skinny with short hair and dark brown skin like Crystal. He smiled through blue braces. I had never seen him before.

"Hey yourself!" I said.

"What's up?" the boy asked. "What's your name?"

I just looked at him. I hadn't asked *his* name. The last thing I needed now was a nosy neighbor.

"I'm living with my grandparents for a while. What grade are you?" the boy asked. Apparently, he was too stupid to get the hint that I didn't want to talk.

I knew Dr. and Mrs. Cohen who lived next door but never paid much attention to them. They were a lot older than my parents. I had heard that the Cohen's children had grown up and moved away. Once in a while, I'd see Dr. and Mrs. Cohen planting vegetables or flowers or sitting in their back yard. They'd say 'Hi' when I walked by. I would answer 'Hi' back, but that was about all I ever said to them.

I just stared at the boy. He didn't look like the Cohen's. Why was he talking to me? Like I cared where he went to school. *What a dork!*

"You're weird," the boy said, shaking his head.

"Back at ya'!" I said and turned without looking back. I walked up the steps to our house and yanked open the front door. Great, I thought. He'll probably be a buddy for Chad and Connor, and right next door. *Yuchh!*

"Is that you, Carrie?" Mom asked. "Please check on your brother. I think he's up to something. I need to rest."

And now, I had to take care of my little brother. That really, REALLY sucked! Big time!

I peeked into Kevin's room expecting to see a disaster area. Instead, I found Kevin sitting on the floor quietly playing with his action figures.

"Carrie," he said. Kevin ran towards me and hugged me tight. "Play with me," Kevin said.

"Okay," I said. "But first, let me unpack my backpack." I threw my backpack and extra clothes in my room. Then I knocked softly on Mom's door.

"Kevin's okay," I said softly. I wasn't sure if I should open the door.

"Thanks for checking," Mom said. Her voice sounded weak, not like the mother I used to know.

"What's the matter?" I asked, suddenly feeling my stomach knot up again. "Are you sick?"

"Just watch your brother, okay?" Mom asked. "I just need to rest a little more." Her voice trailed off.

I felt a little pin prick in my stomach, then another and another. I didn't think Mom sounded 'okay.' It wasn't 'okay' that she was always so tired. It wasn't okay that she always wanted to rest, but I turned and went back to my room.

Kevin was jumping on my bed.

"Piggy back ride," he said. "Piggy rides, all over the house." I sighed. It was going to be a long day.

After giving Kevin three piggyback rides, four horseback rides, and two jumping monkey rides, we played 'Five little monkeys jumping on the bed.' Then Kevin pulled out *Candy Land* and *Chutes and Ladders*. We played until I couldn't stand those games a second longer. I made Kevin a peanut butter and jelly sandwich for lunch and remembered to cut the bread diagonally, cutting off the crusts, the way Kevin liked it. Kevin gobbled his sandwich up and I gave him a glass of milk. Then, I made myself a turkey sandwich and sat down.

"Mommy!" Kevin said and jumped out of his chair, knocking over his milk. Kevin ran and jumped into Mom's arms as she stepped into the kitchen. Mom picked Kevin up and hugged him tightly.

"How's my little sweetie?" she asked brightly but I could see her eyes were teary.

I started wiping up the spilled milk with a dishtowel.

"You'll need a wet rag," Mom said, giving Kevin another hug.

I finished wiping the table and floor then sat down to finish my sandwich. Somehow, I could feel Mom looking at me.

"Cami's mother told me your teacher was leaving. Maybe you'll get a better teacher now."

"Whatever," I said. I didn't look up. "Can I go now?"

Out of the corner of my eye, I saw Mom nod. Mom looked pale and her eyes seemed dull. She seemed like a shadow of the mother I used to know. I felt the pinpricks start again in my stomach. I put my dishes in the dishwasher, went upstairs to my room, and closed the door. Then, I threw myself into the blankets on my bed. I buried my head face down, deep into my pillow, as deep as I could go.

"Good catch," a man said from beyond my window. I lifted my head and looked outside. Dr. Cohen was throwing baseballs at the boy I had met in their backyard. The snow had melted but the grass was brown.

Yucchh. A dork who plays baseball in the winter. A real freak.

Dr. Cohen threw fastballs, grounders, some to the left, some to the right, some right at the boy. He caught them all, no matter how hard Dr. Cohen threw them.

"Okay, let's try some pitching," Dr. Cohen said, dusting off a Frisbee they were using as home plate. I watched the boy put his left foot forward and wind up. I saw a piercing look in his eyes and could almost feel how hard he was concentrating. I knew that look and the feeling that went with it, like you're putting your whole self into the game. It was the look of an athlete who meant business.

The boy threw the ball dead center over the Frisbee. I heard a loud thwack as the ball struck Dr. Cohen's glove.

"Ow," Dr. Cohen cried out wincing. "Not bad."

I threw myself back on my bed and into my pillow. I remembered when my dad had tried to get me interested in Tee Ball and softball. I never liked either one. My dad and I would mostly practice soccer but sometimes we would play volleyball and make up Frisbee games. I remembered the time we went camping on a lake and canoed to a little island. As the sun set, we pitched our tent, cooked some burgers over a crackling fire, roasted marshmallows ...

* * * * *

"Carrie, Carrie," Mom said softly. I jerked my head up from my pillow.

"What time did you girls stay up to? You've been sleeping for three hours."

I buried my face back into my pillow.

"Don't you want to get some fresh air?" Mom asked.

"Okay," I mumbled into the pillow.

Mom's voice turned harder now. "There aren't going to be any more sleepovers if it means you end up wasting the whole next day."

"Okay!" I said lifting my head up just enough to spit the words out. "I'm getting up!" I felt the anger rise in my voice as my stomach tightened. I was ready to argue with Mom. I was ready to yell and scream. But when I sat up, Mom had already left the room.

I put on my sneakers, grabbed my coat and went outside.

"Carrie," Dr. Cohen said. "I'd like you to meet my grandson, David. He's going to be staying with us through the summer."

"We've met," I said, frowning just a little at David to show that I was still annoyed.

"David's parents are working for the next six months in Africa. He will be finishing school this year at Bartonsville. I think he may be in the same grade as you."

I just stared at David.

Mrs. Cohen stepped out of the front door.

"How about a snack?" she asked, "Carrie, please come and join us." She was holding a tray of freshly baked chocolate chip cookies. I could smell chocolate and cookie dough across the yard. I found myself following after Dr. Cohen and David. It's pretty hard to resist chocolate chip cookies, even when you're mad.

"What are your parents doing in Africa?" I asked David as I sat down at the Cohen's kitchen table. I could be polite for chocolate chip cookies.

"They're doctors." David said. "Setting up a new hospital in Ethiopia. Teaching other doctors. Someday, I'm going back there. That's where I was born." He munched on a cookie.

"Cool," I said, grabbing one myself. I felt the chocolate melt in my mouth and a warm feeling inside despite the chill in the air.

"Do you like the cookies?" Mrs. Cohen asked.

"Love 'em," I said and looked eagerly at the plate of cookies.

Mrs. Cohen nodded. "You can have another." Then, she turned to Dr. Cohen and David, "And, you two, don't eat more than two. Dinner's at 6:00."

Dr. Cohen and David nodded silently as they savored their cookies.

"Sounds good," Dr. Cohen said and took another cookie. He turned to me. "Do you want to play some soccer with us? We've just set up a couple nets and could use another player. I'm pretty worn out."

"Okay," I said, getting up. I put my coat back on and headed outside. David followed me out the door. I walked swiftly over to the soccer ball. With one kick, I sent it sailing into the net 40 feet away.

David kicked the ball out of the net and headed towards me. I intercepted him midway across the yard and with a few deft kicks, the ball was mine again and soon flying back into the unguarded net. Soccer was my game and I could hold my own against anyone, from anywhere.

David got the ball again and headed towards me, faking a move to the right, and then moving left. I stole it again. *So easy!* "Boo-yah," I said and once again sent the ball soaring into the net.

"Woo-hoo!"

I was feeling good again, more like my old self every time I kicked the ball.

I could see that David did not like being shown up in his own back yard. He puckered his face in a funny way and tried to get past me another time. This time, he tried to run faster, tripped over the ball, and stumbled, almost falling on his face. He was getting flustered and I loved it. The same thing happened the next time he had the ball, only this time he fell on his butt.

"Awesome!" I shouted.

He looked a little mad now. I loved that even more.

David played okay, just not as good as me. I was killing him in soccer. He also seemed okay with his parents leaving him. That seemed strange but at least he knew where his parents were and what his parents were doing. The next time I stole the ball, I kicked it even harder and soon had another goal.

David was getting frustrated trying to kick the ball past me. But that didn't mean he deserved any mercy. The soccer ball was soon mine once again. I kept scoring goal after goal until Mom called me back home for dinner.

"Welcome to Bartonsville," I said as I ran home.

CHAPTER 7

A new teacher

The first thing I noticed when I got to school was that David was being led to the back of the classroom by a short, thin woman with brown hair. He was given a desk near Connor, Chad, and Crystal. I could see Connor staring at David and then winking at Chad.

I saw a question printed in huge bold letters on the blackboard. It read: *What is a hero?* Ms. Craddick never asked her students questions like that. I remembered Crystal telling me, "That's because she doesn't know the answers. If she can't find a simple answer in the teacher's manual then she won't talk about it."

Ms. Pratt, the school's new principal, walked into the classroom as the bell rang. Ms. Pratt was a rather short woman. Her face was light brown and framed by gray hair. My grandma once told me that every wrinkle stood for a worry. If that was true, Principal Pratt must've had hundreds. She looked much older than any teacher I had ever had and she always looked serious. I had never seen her smile or laugh since she came last year, not even with another teacher.

"Take your seats everyone," Ms. Pratt said. "I want to introduce Ms. Kramer, your new teacher. Ms. Kramer used to teach fifth grade at Bartonsville and she is returning to be your substitute teacher through the end of this school year. I'll be coming in now and then, as well, to help her."

Ms. Kramer walked to the front of the classroom.

"I understand from Principal Pratt that we have a lot to cover in the next four months. I know we will be working hard and I hope we can also have a little fun along the way." Her voice was firm and steady but also warm. Her eyes sparkled behind her glasses.

"Look around you. You'll see a few things are different." Over the blackboard, I saw a large blue pennant with 'University of Michigan' printed in bright gold letters. To the right, I noticed a large picture of an old man with a wrinkled face and flowing white hair. Under the picture, it said, "Imagination is more important than knowledge. For knowledge is limited, whereas imagination embraces the entire world—Albert Einstein."

There was also a new map of the world, one of those maps that I had learned showed the true size of countries, the way you would see them from outer space. So, Africa looked huge while Europe looked strangely small. And there were other new posters all around the room, each with bright colors that seemed to wake up the drab classroom walls.

"I left your desks where they were for today," Ms. Kramer said. "After school today, Mr. Fricter and I are going to move your desks into study groups of four rather than the rows you've had. So, I'm going to need your help. Please take one sheet of the construction paper Mr. Fricter is passing out. Fold it in half from the top to the bottom. And write your full name as large as you can on the lower half." Ms. Kramer demonstrated folding the paper as she spoke. "At the end of class today, put your name on your desk and you will be able to find it easily tomorrow."

"Now, who'd like to tell me the rules of this class?" Ms. Kramer asked.

Chad's hand shot up and Ms. Kramer nodded towards him. "Listen and learn," he said with a sweet smile. Chad then turned and smiled at Principal Pratt who stood by the side of the room.

Ms. Kramer nodded again. "Using our ears certainly helps. What else helps us learn besides listening?"

No one said anything. Ms. Kramer looked at the students, one by one, row by row. I could see that she had a strong look. A few seconds went by, then a minute, then another. Ms. Kramer didn't seem to mind that the clock was ticking and no one was saying a word. Ms. Kramer just kept on looking at each student, one by one.

When Ms. Kramer looked at me, I raised my hand.

"Questions," I said, surprising myself.

"Excellent," Ms. Kramer said. "Questions. Learning isn't easy. It means opening our minds to new things and using our minds to figure things out. And it takes work. You have to do things to learn."

Ms. Kramer looked at each student again. "And we have to have certain rules in this class to make it safe for everyone to learn." Ms. Kramer helped the class put together a list of rules about 'Respect and Responsibility in Classroom 5D.' I know it sounds dorky, but a strange thing happened. Kids started talking in class. Ms. Kramer wrote their ideas on a large sheet of paper with a bold marker and taped it on the wall.

"We can add to these if we need to," she said. "This is a very good start."

"Now, I'm not the only new person in the classroom today. I'm sure you've noticed that we have a new boy and I'd like to introduce Davit Cohen. Davit just moved into our town and he will be with us for the rest of the school year."

"I go by David."

"Then so shall we," Ms. Kramer said. "Okay, time to get to work students. For our writing project today, I'd like you to answer the question on the board. We're going to start a new project, The Heroes Project. In tough times, people think about heroes. Who are some of your heroes? And by heroes, I mean, women and men, boys and girls."

A dozen hands shot into the air. Voices of boys and girls who had hardly spoken all year now rang out clear and proud. It was as if the class had woken from a trance.

"My father is a fireman. He once saved three people from a fire."

"My aunt is a doctor. She saves people's lives in the E.R."

"Luke Skywalker," Alex shouted. Alex was a short boy with brown curly hair and freckles. He looked like he should be in third grade and someone had mixed up his birth date. Alex read every book he could get his hands on about *Star Wars* and seemed to know every word in every one of the movies.

"Great examples," Ms. Kramer said. "I can feel 'the force' growing in our classroom, the Heroes' Force. Now, what makes each of them a hero?"

"It's a person who saves someone else," a boy said.

"It's someone you can look up to," a girl said, "like my grand-mother. She raised my mother and my seven aunts and uncles all by herself. And she did it while she worked three jobs."

"Do heroes have to succeed?" Ms. Kramer asked. "If they fail sometimes, does that mean they aren't a hero?"

"A hero is someone who takes risks to help other people, even when they can get in trouble," Crystal said and she looked at me.

"I think it's someone who cares enough to tell the truth," I said. "Someone you can depend on to say what's real, and not be fakin' it, ever."

"Very nice." Ms. Kramer's eyes seemed to twinkle, as she looked at Crystal and then me. "Telling the truth takes a lot of courage, especially in hard times. What are some other special qualities that heroes show?"

"Kindness," a girl said. "Caring about someone else."

"The guts to act, when other people are afraid," a boy said.

Ms. Kramer nodded.

"Very good. Some people may think it's easier to live with hard-ships and get used to them while others do something about it, even if it means taking risks. What are some of the special skills that heroes use to help them?"

"Skill with a light saber," Alex said. He looked like he was about to jump out of his chair.

"And how did Luke Skywalker learn his skills? How did he become a Jedi knight?" Ms. Kramer asked.

"Obi-Wan and Yoda trained Luke," Alex said. Then he pretended to be Obi-Wan telling Luke to broaden his powers by using his feelings and to trust that 'the force' would remain with him forever.

A couple of the boys laughed while several girls shook their heads and frowned. Everyone knew that once Alex got going with *Star Wars*, he would never stop. But Ms. Kramer went along with Alex.

"Every hero learns from other people. Just like in *Star Wars*, Jedi's train apprentices. And what did Yoda teach about getting angry and letting your hate grow?"

"To never give in to anger. Hatred can pull you into the 'dark side'," David said. The whole class turned to look at him.

"Right," Ms. Kramer said. "In *Star Wars*, Yoda was teaching Luke what it meant to become a hero. And Luke had to practice, every day. Does anybody here play basketball?"

Half the class raised their hands.

"How about baseball or softball?" Again, half the class raised their hands.

"Or, play a musical instrument?" Cami and another six students raised their hands.

"Think about how you learned to play. Did anyone help you? Were you able to watch someone else and get help from them? How much did you have to practice? It's the same for the people we often think about as heroes."

Ms. Kramer walked over to the blackboard and began writing with bright yellow chalk under the question *What is a hero?*

What special skills does your hero use?
How did they learn these skills? Who helped them learn?
What was your hero fighting to achieve?
What was one heroic thing your hero did?

"Okay, I think, Yoda also said, 'Do or do not.'[1] Did I get that right, Alex?" Ms. Kramer asked. Alex nodded.

"So, it's time for all of you to *do* something today to start our series on heroes, our Heroes' Project. Every week, we will be looking at different heroes and what we can learn from them. And then we will find out how those heroes fit in with what we will be learning that week in reading, math, science, and social studies."

Ms. Kramer looked over at Alex.

"For this week's writing assignment, I want you to write about someone you think is a hero. Pick someone who lots of people know, like a movie or sports star, a singer or even a character from a book or movie like Luke Skywalker. Then, answer the four questions I've written on the board. Write about what that person or character did that made them a hero for you and what helped them succeed."

Ms. Kramer looked at each of the students, one by one.

"I'll be looking to see what heroes mean to you and also how well you can write. Heroes do more than talk, so let's get to work."

Principal Pratt left the room and the class worked on their papers until it was time to line up for gym. I was one of the first students back in the classroom after gym. As I sat down, I noticed Chad pick up his math book and walk towards the back of the room. As he passed David's desk, I saw him place his book over David's papers, then quickly lift the book and head to the back of the room and the garbage can. Three papers fluttered downward into the garbage can as Chad turned and stopped by Connor's desk.

Connor smirked and Chad grinned back. Then Connor gave Chad a 'high five.' David was one of the last students to come into the room and didn't see what had happened.

"Okay, class," Ms. Kramer said. "You can take the next 20 minutes to continue working on your papers and then finish them as homework that will be due this Friday. And, Chad, I believe you have something to give to David. Chad will be writing two papers after school in detention this week. One paper on why it's important not to steal, and another one on respecting other students' property."

Ms. Kramer's eyes took on a hard look as she faced Chad. "Stealing papers is a violation of Class Rule #3." Then, she gave the same look to Connor. "Trying to get another student in trouble is a violation of Class Rule #7. Okay, class, get to work."

Chad ran over to the garbage can and pulled out David's stolen papers.

"And, Chad, now would be a good time to start making up for violating the class rules to David and the rest of the class," Ms. Kramer said. "Anything you want to say?" Chad started to shake. He looked at Connor then he pinched his lips tight and shook his head, 'no.'

"Then, I guess you will be writing a third paper this week," Ms. Kramer said, her eyes drilling into Chad. "A paper on how you will make this up to the class. One thing heroes know is that hurting one person hurts everyone. And all three papers need to be signed by your parents, Chad. You have a lot of work to do. Get started."

Chad's jaw dropped so far it looked like it might drag his chin into the floor. And his hands shook so much he dropped his math book after he returned the stolen papers to David's desk. Chad got down on his knees in front of David to pick up his book while David just looked at him with a steady, calm expression on his face. Then, Chad scampered back to his own desk.

Meanwhile, Connor looked like he was in shock. His eyes were bulging out of his face. His mouth hung wide open. He looked ridiculous.

"Awesome," I almost said out loud. I wondered if school could become a good place again. I remembered liking school before Ms. Craddick and Mr. Fricter. For some reason, I thought of my first-grade teacher, Miss Kaplan. She had a cheerful laugh and flowing brown hair. Miss Kaplan used to lead the class in songs along with teaching us to read and do simple arithmetic. She used to stroke my hair when she stopped by my desk to check my work, just a light touch that made my hair flutter and let me know she cared. Then Miss Kaplan would give me a special smile that made me feel warm, deep inside, warm and good.

Just then, Mr. Fricter brushed by my desk, almost knocking my books and papers onto the floor. He stared at me silently and pointed his index finger at my unfinished paper. I felt my face tighten up again. I had almost forgotten Mr. Fricter was still in the classroom. I tried to make myself write my paper, but my eyes followed Mr. Fricter to the back of the classroom. He sneered and pulled out a red notebook he had been carrying all day. Then, he began writing something in the notebook.

I felt a knot form in my stomach and a twinge of pain like a sharp needle had jabbed me in my gut. My lips tightened and my hand froze. And then, out of nowhere, I felt someone lightly ruffle the back of my hair for just a second. I looked up. It was Ms. Kramer looking down at me. For a second, our eyes met and I saw a little twinkle in her eyes.

"That's a great start," Ms. Kramer said, nodding and looking down at the first page of my paper on heroes. "I'm looking forward to reading your paper and learning how your heroes found the courage to tell the truth."

Note

1 Excerpted from *Star Wars Episode V: The Empire Strikes Back* (Lucasfilm LTD, 1980).

CHAPTER 8

Heroes around the world

All that week, the class worked on their hero stories along with the usual reading, math and science. I wrote about *The Chicks* and how they refused to 'shut up' even when some people threatened them and tried to get fans to stop buying their music or going to their concerts.

Cami wrote about Gandhi, a leader in India who helped Indian people gain freedom with marches and protests. He taught people to stand up for their rights and not back down or fight back, even when they were hit and clubbed by soldiers until they collapsed.

"You must be the change you wish to see in the world," Gandhi said.

Crystal wrote about how we shouldn't take the right to go to school for granted. Malala Yousafzai began speaking out against efforts by the Taliban to close schools for girls in Pakistan when she was my age. She continued to speak out for girls' rights to education despite death threats and being shot on her way home from school at age 15. Yousafzai was awarded the Nobel Peace Prize at the age of 17 and her battle for girls and women to go to school goes on.

David wrote about persevering for what you believe in, even if you are put down by the people you are fighting for. Colonel Abdissa Aga started fighting the Italian army to free Ethiopia from colonial rule as a teenager. He was imprisoned in a concentration camp in Sicily, escaped with another prisoner, and returned to the camp to free all the prisoners. When World War II started, Aga was chosen to lead an international army of partisans including English, French, Ethiopians and Americans and played a major role in defeating the fascist government of Italy. Aga rode triumphantly into Rome as part of the allied armies and later into Berlin after battling German Nazis as a Commander of the British Military Police. Despite his successes, Aga experienced racist attacks and, when he returned to Ethiopia, he was forced to enter a military academy as a cadet because Ethiopian army leaders feared his fame would threaten their positions. In spite of this, Aga continued to fight for Ethiopia. He fought Somali invaders and was eventually promoted to become a colonel and the emperor's bodyguard.

"What else have we learned so far from heroes?" Mrs. Kramer asked.

"Stretch out with your feelings.... Trust in the Force," Alex said in his best Obi-Wan voice.

"Right. So how *do* you *stretch out* with your feelings?" Ms. Kramer asked as she stretched her arms from side to side. "Is it a warm-up exercise, like you do before gym class?"

"It means using all your senses," a girl said.

"It means doing something with your mind and body," Cami said. "Like when my mother does yoga. She says it calms her mind down. She can focus better and appreciate things."

"A batter comes to the plate. He uses all his senses," David said. "He watches for clues that the pitcher is going to throw a fast ball or a curve. A great batter uses balance and concentration to knock the ball out of the park."

"What senses help your heroes?" Ms. Kramer asked.

"My dog uses his nose. He's a hero to my family," Liam said. "He warned us when our old house caught on fire. He saved our lives."

"What about taste?" Ms. Kramer asked, "Don't we use taste to know if something is safe to eat? Hearing, touch, sight, smell, and taste. Heroes use all of them to know what's happening, to stay safe, to overcome obstacles, to get through 'tough times.' We can learn from them. Our senses can warn us of danger, like Liam's dog. Our senses can also help us find ways to escape or make our lives safer."

Ms. Kramer turned to the class.

"Now, for the next part of our Heroes' Project, I'd like each of you to write a report about a hero and how they faced hardships and challenges. What helped them overcome the 'tough times' they faced? What helped them keep going, even when other people told them they should give up and stop fighting for what they believed in?"

The class played softball during gym that day. Crystal hit a line drive deep into center and made it to first base. Then I whacked the ball into right field far enough to get a single, putting Crystal on second. Alex and Ted struck out. Then David stepped up to bat. Connor was pitching and threw the first ball right at his chest. David jumped back but returned, just as fast, to the plate. Connor threw another ball, this time aimed at David's head.

"Hey!" I yelled at Connor. The gym teacher looked up from her smart phone. She was probably texting her boyfriend.

"Just warming up the batter," Connor said. He grinned at Chad who was guarding third base and then threw his next pitch. This time David hit the ball deep into center field. I could see the center fielder still chasing after the ball. Crystal ran home as I headed for third base. Chad stuck out his foot to try to trip me but I neatly side-stepped his foot, rounded third, and dashed across home plate. It was 'Easy Peasy,' as my grandma used to say. Two runs. I felt great.

The gym teacher blew her whistle and the class followed her back into the school building.

"Awesome," Cami called out.

She ran over to join Crystal and me and we celebrated with our three-sided fist bump and our fist-bump power-tower then turned towards the school building. Out of the corner of my eye, I noticed David was walking towards the back of the school.

"Something's up," I said and followed after him. Cami and Crystal joined me.

When we got to the back of the building, I saw Chad and Connor standing over Alex. Alex was lying on his side on the grass clutching his stomach. Connor was smacking the softball bat hard on the ground near Alex's head.

"Strike three," Connor hissed. "I do believe you're out."

"Where's your light saber now?" Chad asked with a wicked laugh.

"Maybe you should trust in my bat today, young Jedi," Connor said sounding more like Mr. Fricter than Darth Vader. "Feel the power of the bat," he said as he smacked the ground again closer to Alex's head.

"Looks like you and Ms. Kramer are getting to be real good *Star Wars* buddies. So, I'm sure you won't mind helping us out. Let's *see*. What could you do for us this week? What do you think, Connor?" Chad asked. "Maybe our Jedi knight here could use 'the Force' to do our math homework for us. Give us the answers each day."

"And maybe he could give us that little gift we were talking about last week," Connor said with a wicked grin. "You wouldn't want Chad and me to go without dessert at lunch today." Connor put on his fake pout. I wanted to kick him.

"Forget the ball?" David asked in a low but firm voice. Chad and Connor jerked themselves around and saw David standing behind them, gently tossing the ball up in the air from hand to hand. Alex quickly scooted away while Connor lifted up his bat, pointing it now at David.

"I've got the bat, 'new boy.' And I don't think I can miss," Connor said.

David put the ball in his right hand and I could see his eyes take on the same piercing look I had seen a few days before. David shifted his weight, putting his left foot forward and started to pull his right arm back.

"Looks like we've got company," Chad said, spotting Cami, Crystal and me coming closer.

"Hey, Dim-wat, that's your name, right? Dim-wat or is it Dim-wit? I see your girlfriends have come to save you. Just in time," Connor said. He pointed his bat at David again then turned to Chad, "Out of here, Bro." Then, they ran back towards the building.

"You okay?" I asked as I ran over to Alex.

Alex nodded, standing up and dusting off his pants. "I wish I did have a light saber. I'd cut off their heads."

"They're not worth the trouble," I said softly. "They're just jerks."

"Cockroaches," Cami said.

"That's putting it nicely," Crystal said. "I have a few names I could use. First one starts with A ..."

"There's always a couple jerks like that in every school," David said.

"You guys ..." Alex started to say, but he was interrupted by Mr. Fricter yelling from the corner of the building.

"I heard some of my class were late getting back from gym. Looks like you'll all be *late* getting home from school today."

Mr. Fricter glared at me.

"Party's over. Get moving! Every minute you're late is another ten minutes I get after school." Then Mr. Fricter grinned with the left side of his mouth curled up higher than the right side. He turned on his heel and marched back into the building.

I usually felt my gut cringe when Mr. Fricter grinned at me with that horrible look. But strangely, this time, it didn't bother me to be in trouble or even to get another detention.

"You know, Alex, I think you're right," I said, looking at my friends as we walked back. "'The Force' *is* all around us."

CHAPTER 9
The secrets of heroes

Over the next six weeks, Ms. Kramer asked the class to share more of what they had learned about the secrets of heroes. We talked about what helped heroes, the mistakes they made and how they fought to help others. Then, Ms. Kramer used the stories of these heroes to make learning science and math a little more fun. For science, Ms. Kramer talked about how Charles Darwin used his studies and observations to shape and re-shape his understanding of how animals evolved. I knew that. What I didn't know was that Darwin grappled with fears that his theories would lead him to be branded and attacked as a non-believer and lose the love of his wife.

For math, Ms. Kramer used the story of Florence Nightingale, the Lady with the Lamp, who cared for British troops in the Crimean War and was known as the founder of modern nursing. In the 1800s, a woman could only become a nurse or a teacher. I learned that Nightingale was also a skilled mathematician and invented the pie charts used in statistics around the world. She used math to convince government leaders to provide better health care and helped the U.S. army in the Civil War.

For social studies and reading, Mrs. Kramer shared how Nelson Mandela was inspired by a British poet to persevere despite decades of brutal imprisonment and remain 'master of my fate' and 'captain of my soul.'[1] Mandela never gave up on his belief that the people of South Africa could come together, black and white.

"What keeps your heroes safe?" Ms. Kramer asked one Monday.

"Using all their senses," a boy said, "to warn them of danger, like Spiderman feeling something with his spider senses."

"Special skills they learn with practice, like pitching a curve ball or making a three-point swoosh, hitting only net," David said, pretending to sink a free throw from his chair.

"Knowing they can get help and who can help them," Crystal said.

"Is it okay for heroes to ask for help?" Ms. Kramer asked.

"My coach says that a team is always stronger than one player," a boy responded.

"Soldiers work as a team. It can mean the difference between winning a battle or getting killed," another boy said.

"Now, for today's writing assignment," Ms. Kramer said, "I want you to think about your own *Secrets of Staying Safe*. Write about how you used your senses to protect yourself and other people and how you got help for yourself. We'll talk about this later in the week. In the meantime, let's see what we can learn from the heroes you've been studying."

Crystal talked about how Harriet Tubman was born a slave but from childhood she protected other people, even when it led to her getting hurt as a teenager. As an adult, she made 19 trips into states with slavery, risking her life. She guided over 300 slaves to freedom. Harriet Tubman called herself a 'conductor' on the Underground Railroad and was proud that she never lost a 'passenger'.

"Do heroes have to be perfect?" Ms. Kramer asked.

"No way," a boy said. "It's like Pokemon or Superman and kryptonite. Everybody has a weakness."

"Can they make themselves perfect?"

"No one's ever perfect," Crystal said. "Real heroes admit when they are wrong."

Alex talked about how John F. Kennedy became a war hero. He told Americans to 'ask not what your country can do for you, ask what you can do for your country.' Before he could become president, he had to show Americans they didn't have to be afraid of having a Catholic president. President Kennedy inspired many people but he also agreed to a plan for the United States to invade Cuba and many people died. Kennedy had the courage to tell the world how he had been wrong to do this.

David described how many people thought Michael Jordan was the greatest basketball player, ever. But the first time he tried out for a school basketball team, the coach didn't pick him. He was also taunted by other kids for being black and he wanted to fight those kids. His father told him to 'rise above' the kids who tried to put him down. And that's just what he did, jumping high above everyone else on the basketball court.

It was time for lunch. Ms. Kramer collected everyone's reports and had them copied into booklets she passed out the next day for every student to read after completing a math lesson.

I thought a lot about the stories of presidents that students had written. President Kennedy stood with the people of Berlin, Germany, who were cut off from supplies and the rest of Germany. President Kennedy pledged that Americans would support the Berliners, risking war with the Soviet Union to stand up for the rights of people who had been seen as enemies a generation before.

President H.W. Bush volunteered to serve his country as one of the youngest navy pilots in World War II instead of going off to college. He flew 68 missions before his plane was hit and caught on fire. He climbed out of the plane and the wind blew him into the tail of the plane gashing his head and bruising his eye before he parachuted into the ocean. Bush managed to inflate a life raft and paddled as hard as he could to avoid drifting onto an island controlled by the Japanese army. He was rescued by a submarine while his two-man crew perished. Other airmen were killed by the Japanese army. From that day forward, he thought about his lost crewmen and he devoted his life to public service as a way to give something back to the country he loved. Bush was a war hero like President Kennedy and called for Americans to become a 'thousand points of light,' helping those in need. Years later, as an older man, he parachuted from airplanes to celebrate his birthdays, repeating in a way his narrow escape from death as a young man. Jumping out of an airplane sounded crazy-brave, something I would never do.

I also learned that presidents struggled with problems in their own families. President Clinton lost his father as a boy, and as a teenager, he stood up to his stepfather, an alcoholic, and stopped his stepfather from hurting his mother. President Obama felt abandoned by his father as a child, and, as a young man, he worked to put the different pieces of his life together so he could become a 'whole' person. He learned how he was linked to the struggles of both sides of his family, to his white mother and his mother's parents who had raised him in Hawaii, and also to his black father and his father's family in far-away Kenya. Obama risked losing a second term as president by fighting for all Americans to have health care insurance so they could see doctors whether they were rich or poor, healthy or already sick. He described true courage coming from an understanding of who we really were, then going deep to pull out the best in ourselves and do hard things that would help others. Nice words, I thought, but who are we?

Presidents Bush and Obama received awards for their courage but I kept thinking about the story I learned of a humble soldier in World War II, Master Sergeant Roddie Edmonds. This soft-spoken man was not a president or prime minister, a famous sports star or singer, a king or a knight. He came back from the war and wouldn't talk about what happened like so many other soldiers. After he died, his son read his diary and learned that his father had been imprisoned by the Nazis with most of his soldiers in a camp where prisoners were starved. The German commandant ordered Edmonds to have only the Jewish-American soldiers report for the next morning's assembly. Instead, Edmonds ordered all of the Americans to assemble. The commandant rushed towards Edmonds, put his pistol against Edmonds' head and demanded that Edmonds identify the Jewish soldiers. Edmonds responded "We are all Jews here" and told the commandant that if he wanted to kill the Jewish soldiers, he'd have to shoot all of the prisoners because they knew who he was and he would be prosecuted for war crimes after the war ended. The commandant backed down. Because of his courage, Edmonds saved over 200 men who would have been sent off to slave labor camps with little chance of survival. Sergeant Edmonds never stood up on a stage and received an award for what he did. He just did what he felt was right to save his men. I wondered if I would have had the courage to do the same thing.

On Friday, Ms. Kramer asked the class to hand in their papers on the *Secrets of Staying Safe* and to share what they had learned.

"Do heroes get scared?" Ms. Kramer asked.

"Everyone gets scared," a girl said. "Everybody."

"Not me," Connor boasted. He grinned at Chad and Chad grinned back.

"It's part of being human," Cami said.

"Can fears help us?" Ms. Kramer asked.

"They warn you of danger," Alex said.

"My dad says fear gives us energy, like when you step up to the plate," Liam said, his voice rising in pitch, "and the bases are loaded in the last game of the World Series!"

"But it can hurt us too," I said. "People can get too scared to do anything."

"Great points," Ms. Kramer nodded.

"So what helps heroes get past their fears?" Ms. Kramer asked.

"If you accept fear as natural, then you can use it," Cami said.

"How?" Ms. Kramer asked.

"You can use fears as a signal that it's time to do something," a girl said.

"Have you ever noticed that it's easier to walk steadily up a steep hill and keep moving forward than to try to stand still on the side of the hill?" Ms. Kramer asked. "Test it out. Try it, the next time you walk up a really steep hill."

"Or, if you're skiing, it's easier to make a turn with speed, than to try to turn slowly," a boy said.

"In choir, I know it's easier to hit the right notes if you sing louder, than if you sing softly," a girl said.

Ms. Kramer turned to the class.

"For next week's paper, I'd like you to write another story about heroes. This time, ask someone in your family about their heroes. It can be a parent, a grandparent, a brother, a sister, or a cousin, or even a very close family friend. Ask them to tell you how their hero used her/his senses to watch out for danger? What were some of the special skills this hero used? Who helped this hero develop their special skills? What was your hero fighting to achieve? What were some of the things this hero did to make things better for other people? What is one lesson we can learn from this hero?"

The school intercom came on and the school secretary said, "Ms. Kramer, please report to the principal's office."

"Okay, students, please start on your math and vocabulary homework until the bell," Ms. Kramer said and then left the class.

Out of the corner of my eye, I saw Chad winking at Connor. Then, Chad slowly got out of his seat with his sad, lost little boy look on his face and his math paper in his hand. Chad walked over to Mr. Fricter who was sitting at Ms. Kramer's desk at the front of the room. I could hear Chad asking for help in his fake, little boy's voice as he blocked Mr. Fricter's view of the center of the class. Quickly, I began tapping the C code on my desk, just loud enough for Cami and Crystal to hear.

I turned to look around the room and my eyes met up with Cami who sat over to the right of me towards the front of the classroom. Together, we both turned to the back of the classroom, just as Crystal began turning to the left. All of the girls saw Connor's hand sneaking over towards Crystal's back. He was holding a book and something I couldn't see. His face was the picture of sweetness and innocence.

Connor looked up. He saw three girls staring right at him. Six eyes burned into him like laser beams. I was half-way out of my chair. Connor's eyes started to bulge out and his jaw dropped. His mouth seemed to be saying, "what the ...?" but no sound came out. Connor quickly pulled his hand back and bent his head down, pretending to look at his book.

It works, I thought, sitting back down. The Three Cs could stop Chad and Connor.

Note

1 Excerpts from *Invictus* by William Ernest Henley. Henley became ill with tuberculosis at age 12 and as a young man faced the agonizing choice of amputating his leg or risking death after tuberculosis spread to his foot. While imprisoned on Robben Island, Nelson Mandela recited the poem to other prisoners and was empowered by its message of self-control in spite of afflictions. For the full poem, see: www. poetryfoundation.org/poems/51642/invictus.

CHAPTER 10

Grandma's apple pie

Over the weekend, I asked Mom who her favorite hero was.

"I don't think I really had any heroes growing up," Mom said then paused. Mom's eyes drifted upward and to the right as a dreamy look came over her face, "But now, I'd say my mother."

I saw little tears grow in her eyes.

"I'm sorry, Mom," I said softly. I felt bad for asking but at the same time I was still angry at Mom. And thinking about Grandma somehow made me feel both sad and angry. Mom had cried for weeks after Grandma died. That was two years ago. Dad had just started working out of town most of the time. And that meant I had to take care of Kevin and do most of the cooking and cleaning. It wasn't right. It wasn't fair. And, this last year, Mom had been going into her room and crying again. I missed Grandma too. I just wouldn't let myself cry like Mom did. I wouldn't lock myself away in my room.

Grandma was always special. My Grandpa, Mom's Dad, had died when I was just a baby. My Dad's parents died before I was born. I grew up going to Grandma's house. We went every Sunday for a special Grandma dinner. That always meant a special Grandma dessert like hot baked apple pie with vanilla ice cream, or my favorite, deep dark chocolate cake that was so rich each bite melted in your mouth. That was a cake that warmed your whole body, filled you with energy and made you want to sing out loud. *Yumm!* Just thinking about it made my mouth water.

I remembered how Mom had seemed so happy in those visits, like she could throw off all the stress from her work. I would play in the backyard with Dad while Mom and Grandma talked. But Grandma got sick three years ago, very sick. And soon, she couldn't cook or even live by herself. The visits to Grandma's house stopped. Instead, we would visit Grandma at hospitals and then a place where very sick people lived. I didn't like going there. It felt weird, scary, and smelled bad. I didn't want to stay long in that place but then I felt bad because I wanted to get away and that meant leaving Grandma there. Grandma got thinner and thinner, weaker and weaker. I didn't want to look at her. That made me feel even worse.

I was in the kitchen when Mom got the call that Grandma died. I heard Mom gasp. Tears streamed from her eyes. Mom changed after that. It was like all the joy had been sucked out of her somehow and was buried with Grandma. The lines on her face grew deeper. Her voice changed from loud, strong, full of life to a dull whisper except when she got angry which seemed to become more and more often and usually about something Dad or I did. At night, I'd hear her call out as if she was trapped in a nightmare. It was like she had become a new mom, a mom I hardly knew. Thinking about her made my stomach hurt.

A few months after Grandma died, we moved into Grandma's house. Mom and Dad said it was because it was a better house but I overheard them say it was really because we couldn't afford our own house anymore. Moving into Grandma's house was strange. I kept expecting to see Grandma come into the kitchen or come out of her bedroom. But she wasn't there. I wished again that I could go back to being eight-years-old, *before* Grandma got sick, before the worst things happened.

"It's okay," Mom said sadly. She looked at me and her eyes seemed to brighten just a little. "I'd like to tell you about your grandmother."

I could see the tears growing again in Mom's eyes.

"I can come back. Really, Mom."

"You're a lot like her, you know," Mom said, "kind-hearted and full of spirit. Caring, but tough when it counts. When I grew up, my brothers and I, we all knew, 'Don't cross Mom.' We knew she loved us more than anything in the world, but we also knew we'd better obey her. She and Grandpa pushed us to work hard in school. 'A job worth doing was a job worth doing well.' They both believed that. And that meant studying hard and getting the best grades. And 'Don't mess up Grandma's kitchen.' That was her domain, where she made the rules."

"And the pies and cakes." I felt hungry just thinking about them.

"Yes, pies and cakes and every holiday meal. But there was more to your grandmother than that. I didn't see it growing up. I guess I was too busy doing my own thing. And, as a teenager, I was too busy getting angry at all my parents' rules. It seemed like they gave me more limits than my brothers, like when I had to be home, or who I could go out with. I always felt it was so unfair, even though my brothers were older. Everything seemed to come easy to them, good grades, being chosen for school sports, lots of friends. Teachers loved my brothers, while everything seemed to be hard for me."

Mom shook her head slowly.

"I thought Grandma and Grandpa expected me to do the same things as my brothers. And I couldn't. So, I got mad, mad at myself, and then mad at them. And since Grandma was the one around most of the time, I got mad at her most of all."

Mom sighed.

"Mostly, I didn't want Grandma to know how I wasn't doing as well as my brothers did. Every '75' on a test, every 'Needs Improvement' note from a teacher made me wish Grandma wasn't there to shake her head and give me that long look that made me cringe inside. I didn't want her around. I wished she had been working at a job outside our home, like most of my friends' moms. My friends seemed to have more freedom. No one was checking up on every test score or missed class.

"I didn't think I could ever do what Grandma expected me to do. I hated those looks she gave me. And then when I was a teenager,

I got angrier. I pushed her away. She wanted too much! I stayed away from home more and more. I got in some trouble and I kept it to myself. So, Grandma couldn't know. She couldn't help."

"And then, I don't know. Time went by, months, years, when we hardly talked. I went away to college. I made some friends. I met your father. Grandma and I weren't that close anymore. And, for a while, I didn't even realize what had happened. I had your father. We were really good for each other back then. I had my friends."

I thought about my own quizzes and troubles at school, how I didn't want Mom to see my teacher's notes. Mom was looking upwards at the ceiling now. Tears glistened in her eyes.

"She needed me when Grandpa died. I let her down."

I watched the tears streaking down Mom's face. She turned towards me, meeting my eyes.

"I didn't realize how Grandma had given up her own opportunities for my brothers and me. She never went past high school but I knew she was very smart. She was smart about what really mattered."

"You know how I knew?" Mom asked, looking deeper into my eyes. "Because, when I was a kid, somehow she always knew when I really needed help. She always knew when I really needed her. She was always there for the big things. Like when I wanted to blow off chemistry and algebra in high school and forget about going to college, she sat down and worked the problems with me. She made me study. I hated her making me do it but I passed. And, when I had a big crush on this boy and I found him kissing my best friend, I went nuts. But Grandma helped me figure that one out too. Or, when I planned a big party for my friends and found everything was going wrong and nothing looked right. That's when Grandma knew to come."

I could see Mom's eyes getting misty again and I felt tears forming in my eyes too.

"I miss Grandma too," I said. I felt a wave of sadness sweep through me that washed away the 'mad'. I fought to hold my own tears inside. I remembered Grandma's funeral. So many relatives were crying, so many tears. And, at the cemetery, Mom was sobbing. Dad put his arms around Mom. I was crying too at the funeral. I didn't know what to do.

Mom put her arm behind my back and began gently rubbing, round and round, deeper and deeper, spreading circles of warmth. I felt the tension in my back melt away, as if Mom was loosening all the knots in my body. Slowly, one by one, each knot melted away.

"She loved you," Mom said. "Her eyes would light up whenever she saw you. She couldn't help but smile."

"What kept her going, you know, when things got hard?"

"I don't know." Mom looked up again. Her eyes drifted away. "Grandma used to tell me, 'Find what's in your heart, in the quiet space, away from all the craziness in your life. And then you will know what you need to do'." Mom sighed. "But, when Grandpa died, it was like the sparkle went out in her eyes. I thought she'd never recover. He was such a good man, quiet, but always there for all of us. Grandma went into a slump. I'd say to her, 'Tomorrow's a new day,' and some of the same things she used to say to me. But nothing seemed to make her feel better. She'd just cry or go into her room and shut the door. But then," Mom paused and looked at me, "almost like magic, she came back to life."

I looked up. "What happened?"

"I had a baby girl. Grandma loved that baby girl." Mom smiled. It was the first time I had seen Mom smile in so very long. "Grandma picked out her name, Caroline, because it means 'strong.' And we called her 'Carrie'." Mom pulled me close. "And, somehow, after you were born, I got a little smarter. I let Grandma back into my life. We became close again." Mom started to cry. Big, hot wet tears streamed down her face. "I don't think this is what you expected when you asked about heroes.

Grandma wasn't exactly like Hermione or Harry Potter or those singers you like so much."

"I'd rather have a real hero from my family, any day." I felt Mom's tears on my face and the warmth of Mom holding me close. "What happened after I was born?"

"You had a tough time the first few months nursing and sleeping, keeping your food down, getting enough to eat. Some babies are like that. And for those first few months, your father and I were so tired. I didn't know what to do. I got so worn out, I could hardly think. Grandma moved into our apartment. She gave up a new job she liked, moved into our little apartment and slept on the living room couch. Your father and I got some sleep. I'd ask her, 'Mom, do you really want to do this?' She'd just look at me and say, 'This is what it's all about. There's nothing more important than caring for children.' After a couple months, we got you on a feeding schedule that worked and you just took off."

Mom rubbed my back again, her fingers circling to the left, then circling to the right. "I think Grandma loved how spirited you were. Starting when you were about six months old, you had this little impish grin when you were doing something new, like the first time you went down a slide. You were just eight months old. You closed your eyes tight and then grinned. ;It was the cutest thing! You wanted to do it again and again. Grandma laughed and laughed. I can still see her eyes twinkling."

I remembered Grandma's smile, her laugh, and her twinkling eyes. It made me want to smile myself.

"You know, your great grandmother helped lead marches for women to have the right to vote. And your great grandfather was a union organizer during the Depression. So, you weren't the first in our family to fight to make things better. Grandma loved to see that feisty part of you."

"What do you mean?"

"Oh, like the time you were just two years old. We had taken you to this big public park with fountains, big fountains and a place with little sprinklers that was just perfect for little children to play in. It was a hot summer's day and we let you take off your shoes and wade in the fountain. You were splashing and laughing with a bunch of other little kids. Then this park policeman came up, a really big guy, tall, tough-looking with a loud, deep voice, bulging eyes and oily black hair. He started yelling at the kids in a mean voice, like they were criminals 'endangering the public welfare' or something crazy like that. He acted like he was going to lock all of the little kids up.

"'Get out of the water! Get out of the water, NOW!' the policeman ordered. All the other kids took one look at this big guy in a blue uniform and scampered out of the water as fast as they could go. But you just kept on splashing and splashing. The police officer kept on yelling and you just looked up at him and stared right back with your cute little cheeks pinched in and your hands on your hips. Then, you pressed your little lips together and said 'Not nice' to the officer. Grandma loved that look."

"I was a troublemaker."

"Yes, but a cute one." Mom smiled. "I remember when you were three years old, you always wanted to play with the eight and nine year olds. At the playground, you'd beg your dad and me to go on the high monkey bars like the big kids. We'd tell you it was too high. You could do it when you were eight-years-old. Then you put your hands on your hips. You looked right at us and declared in your loudest voice, 'I'm not scared. I can do it'."

"Did you let me?"

"No way! We told you 'We're scared.' 'Stay on the low bars!' And then we'd catch you sneaking off to the high bars anyway. That's just the way you were. Pushing the limits, always asking 'Why?' when your dad or I set rules. Then challenging whatever we said. 'Another lawyer in the family,' your dad would say. 'Just what we need, another lawyer.' And Grandma would say to your dad,

'Well, what do you expect? You and my daughter, you're both stubborn'." Mom closed her eyes.

Just then, we heard a loud crash. A shiver ran down my spine. It was glass, I knew it somehow. Kevin screamed. Mom raced into the kitchen. I ran after her. A glass bowl lay shattered on the floor with smashed strawberries all around. Kevin was standing there barefoot in the middle of broken shards of glass. He started screaming again when he saw us. Then he stepped on a piece of glass and shrieked.

I felt a hundred pinpricks in my stomach. My head throbbed. Mom quickly picked Kevin up, stepping over the sparkling glass. I saw a large cut on Kevin's knee. Blood was streaking out in what looked like little rivers. Blood was also dripping from his left foot. Kevin looked at his knee and screamed again. Then, he held up his foot and his eyes opened wide. He screamed again and started shaking. Mom swooped him up and hugged him. She kissed his cheek, pressed her cheek into his tears and carried him into the bathroom.

I got the broom and started sweeping shattered glass into a dustpan. I saw little bits of red strawberries, shards of glass and blood, Kevin's blood. I felt more pinpricks in my stomach. I threw the glass into the trash and rinsed the blood off the dustpan. Then, I washed the floor over and over but I kept seeing shards of glass and blood. I kept on washing the floor until my shoulders ached.

That Sunday, Mom baked an apple pie. We didn't have ice cream to put on top but the pie was warm. And the crust was crisp and crumbled just right with just a hint of butter. I lifted a second bite to my mouth. The warm cinnamon smell and sweet taste of apples reminded me of Grandma.

CHAPTER 11
Hot water

On Monday, I was sitting just in front of Chad and Connor on the bus. It was the only seat I could get. Believe me, I would never want to sit anywhere near them! Dark gray clouds hung low overhead. It looked like it might rain any minute. A cold dampness filled the air outside and spread a chill through the bus. I shivered every time the bus door opened.

Chad and Connor were snickering in between whispers to each other. I couldn't hear every word, but I heard enough to make out what they were talking about. Each of their parents had filed a complaint with the school board president about Ms. Kramer.

"She's in trouble now," Chad said.

"I bet that's why Principal Pratt called her down to her office twice last week, probably chewed her out good," Connor said.

"Serves her right for keeping me after school," Chad said. "I hope they fire her."

"They will," Connor said. "My dad says she's got to go if she doesn't knock off this 'heroes' stuff and get back to the stuff she's supposed to be teaching."

"She's a 'goner'," Chad said. "Bye, bye, Ms. Kramer."

"Maybe her 'hero' will come and rescue her," Connor said.

"Right, if she's got one," Chad said. "Maybe Alex and his light saber ..."

"Hey," Connor snickered. "I think our little Jedi owes us ..."

The bus stopped with a loud squeal and four other students got on. After that, I couldn't hear anything but snickers and snorts from the two boys.

I knew someone had to stop them. I felt pinpricks in my stomach. My legs kept jerking wildly. I shuddered thinking about how Principal Pratt might bring back Ms. Craddick. My stomach started to ache.

Cami got on the bus and sat down next to me.

"You look sick," she said with a worried look.

"It's worse," I said, pointing to the boys behind us in a way only Cami could see. "Mega worse." I told her what I had heard.

In the front of the classroom that day, Ms. Kramer had a large glass tank. Inside, a bright green frog was resting on a rock by a miniature pond.

"Today, we're going to learn a lesson from frogs. I borrowed this frog from a friend of mine, a science teacher at the middle school. I want to tell you about a little science experiment, an experiment with frogs from a long time ago. What do you think would happen if you dropped a frog into a pool of very hot water?"

"It would jump out," Crystal said quickly. "It would use its hind legs and jump as far as it could. Frogs can jump very high."

"Don't do it!" Aliesha said. "Don't hurt the frog."

"Don't worry," Ms. Kramer said. "We're not going to hurt the frog. We can learn from what happened in the experiment without repeating it. And Crystal is right. The frog would use its senses to know that the temperature of the water was dangerous. And then the frog would do everything it could to escape. It would squeeze its legs together real hard and jump out of the water. And it would use its strong muscles and webbed feet to push itself up high into the air. Frogs keep themselves safe by jumping away from danger.

"Now," Ms. Kramer asked, "what would happen if we put the frog in a nice pool of cool water, maybe with a few flies buzzing around for the frog to eat?"

"It might swim around, catch a few flies," a boy said smiling.

"And what would happen if the temperature of the water in the pool was increased ever so slowly?" Ms. Kramer asked. "What if the temperature was increased such a tiny bit, so little, the frog would hardly even notice it."

"Probably, nothing," a boy said. "Maybe it would eat another fly."

"And what if we increased the temperature the next day, just another tiny bit?"

"Go about his business. Swim a little. Eat another fly," a girl said. "Enjoy the pool."

"And what if we kept on increasing the temperature of the water by a little tiny bit and the frog didn't notice?" Ms. Kramer asked.

"Maybe the frog would take a nap," a girl said. "Pretend he was in Florida catching the rays, chilling out on the beach."

"Or just relax, pretend he's in a sauna," a boy said, pretending to stretch out in his chair.

All the students were paying close attention now. But I noticed that Mr. Fricter was paying the closest attention of all. In fact, he seemed to be writing down every word Ms. Kramer said in his red notebook. And every couple of minutes, he would look up and check the clock on the wall. I wondered what he was up to. I had never seen him write much at all, not through a hundred of Ms. Craddick's boring lectures.

"The frog should get out of there," Crystal said. "Fast!"

"Yes," Ms. Kramer said. "But, some scientists from the 1800s said that something different happened, something hard to believe.[1]

69

In their experiment, the frog just stayed in the water. The frog stayed in the water until it was so hot that the frog became weaker and weaker and weaker. And then he couldn't jump. He became too weak to escape. He couldn't catch flies. The frog seemed to get used to the water getting hot and didn't know he was in danger until it was too late."

"That's a terrible experiment!" Theresa, a girl in our class cried out. I saw Mr. Fricter writing very fast in his red notebook.

"Some scientists don't think it's true. And we are not going to repeat the experiment to find out," Ms. Kramer said. "We are going to take good care of our frog. We are going to see what lessons our own little frog can teach us. But first, what can we learn from this story? What can we learn that we could use to help ourselves, our friends and our families?"

"Watch what's going on," Alex said. "Use our senses."

"Stay away from mean scientists!" Aliesha said with a nervous smile.

"Remember that things can change," I said. "Good things may not stay good, not forever."

I felt a tear drop growing in my right eye. My lips began to quiver and my chin dropped. My mask was slipping away. *Not now. Not ever. Never ever!* I shook my head left and right and stared hard at the frog. The teardrop melted away.

"People can be smarter than frogs," Ms. Kramer said softly, looking at me. "People can learn from what happened before."

I looked up. I felt my cheeks tighten.

"Sometimes people close their eyes. They can be as blind as the frog in that experiment. They pretend things are okay when they aren't. They close their eyes to what's really happening!" I felt my fists clench onto the top of my desk. My legs began kicking wildly again. I knew my voice had become hard, sharp, loud, angry and

I didn't care. I tightened my lips and pinched my cheeks into my jaw. I pulled my mask on tight.

"That's very true," Ms. Kramer said, looking into my eyes. "People often have a hard time with change. If things were working well a certain way, people often want to keep on doing the same things, even if those ways stop working." She turned and faced the rest of the class.

"It's hard to learn something new. It's hard to try something different. That's where heroes come in. Many of the famous heroes you have written about spoke out for change, even when it meant taking big risks. Every man who signed the *Declaration of Independence* in Philadelphia knew that it meant the British would hang him if he was caught. But, they did it anyway."

"'Give me liberty or give me death'," a boy said.

"Yes, but now, over two hundred years later, how many Americans even know why we have the government we do? Why do we have three branches of government, and what did that have to do with King George and the Revolutionary War?"

"Each branch was supposed to keep the others from taking over total power," Cami said. "Jefferson and Madison wanted to be sure that we didn't end up with a king again."

"Very good," Ms. Kramer said, "and just like Jefferson and the other delegates who risked their lives signing the *Declaration of Independence*, people have always looked for heroes who took risks to stand up against those who would harm other people. These were real people who helped others and sacrificed for the good of all. Moms and dads, grandmas and grandpas, people who never expected to be heroes. They saw a need and they took action. Like the brave firefighters who climbed up the World Trade Tower on 9/11 to save people. Or, parents whose children have grown and now open up their home to take in other children in trouble, children who have no place to live. Or, a lawyer who helps a woman escape from a husband who's hurting her, a doctor who risks catching a deadly disease to save a patient, And boys and girls who help take care of family members who are sick. Real people willing to take risks to help others and not just pretend things are okay or that somebody else will do it.

"This week," Ms. Kramer continued, "I'd like you to think about the lessons frogs can teach us. Think about the frog experiment. What would it take to warn the frog to escape? What warning systems could you put in place to protect a frog from the water getting too hot? And I'd like you to learn more about the heroes your parents, or other family members, admire. What did their heroes watch out for? What warned their heroes to take action? And what kept that hero going when things got tough?

"You can come up, two at a time, to look at the frog and then start reading about frogs in your science book. Think about what makes a frog special. What special strengths does it have? What can it do to escape danger? Later, we'll do our math, reading and social studies, like usual. And we will learn about a frog's senses and body parts. We've got lots to learn. So, let's get going."

The speaker came on in the classroom. Ms. Kramer was called to the office. After she left, students went to look at the frog then returned to their seats. Chad lingered by the frog then followed Connor to the back of the room. I noticed that Connor was holding something and started to tap but there was too much noise in the room. The two boys passed Crystal's desk. Suddenly, Crystal jumped out of her chair screaming, "Snake! Snake!"

I saw Chad and Connor laughing and what looked like a snake was lying behind Crystal's desk.

"Stop it!" I shouted, jumping up.

Mr. Fricter stood up. I could see him wince again and then he pointed his index finger like a sword.

"Quiet!" he roared. "Sit down!"

"But, they ..." Cami cried out.

Mr. Fricter wheeled around, glaring now at Cami. "You too!" he said. His voice was loud, booming, like a cannon blast.

Meanwhile, Chad dropped his book. He bent down to pick up the book and quickly lifted the fake snake off the floor with the book. Then, Chad and Connor turned and walked back to their seats. Their faces were pictures of sweet innocence once again.

"And you," Mr. Fricter said, glaring now at Crystal with his meanest look, "What are you doing out of your chair? Sit down! And STOP SCREAMING IN MY CLASS!"

"But," Crystal started to say.

"BUT NOTHING! SIT DOWN. NOW!"

"She didn't do anything," I shouted.

"Quiet!" Mr. Stricter said, glaring now at me. "That's detention for all three of you, after school today." He pointed his index finger at me, then Cami and then Crystal. Then, he smiled his crooked smile with the left side of his lips reaching up towards his nose. "You three will be writing papers on how important it is to 'Listen and learn.' And a note will be going home to your parents about how you disrupted class today. Bring it back signed tomorrow. Now, all of you, get back to your science books."

Ms. Kramer returned and later that day, Principal Pratt came into the classroom. She stood in the back of the classroom and watched Ms. Kramer teach that week's vocabulary lesson. She left after a few minutes without saying a word but then returned later in the day and stood at the back of the classroom for half an hour. She didn't smile even once. Ms. Kramer was called to the office one more time late in the afternoon and returned just as the bell rang. All the students grabbed their books and headed home except Cami, Crystal and me.

"These three have some extra time to put in," Mr. Fricter said.

"I'll take care of detention today," Ms. Kramer said calmly and sat down at her desk. "I have work to do myself."

As soon as Mr. Fricter left, Crystal ran up to Ms. Kramer's desk.

"Mr. Fricter says you three disrupted the classroom," Ms. Kramer said. "What happened?"

"Connor pinched my back with a snake," Crystal said.

"I saw something on the floor," Cami said. "Then, it was gone."

"I saw something too. It looked like a rubber snake," I said.

"Do you have the snake?" Ms. Kramer asked. "Did anyone else see it?"

The girls shook their heads.

"Please don't send a note home to my parents," Crystal said.

"That's school policy," Ms. Kramer said. "Parents are notified of any detentions. Maybe you can use this time though."

"What do you mean?" Cami asked with a sad look. I didn't think that Cami had ever had a detention in her life before this year. And now in just a few weeks, she had had two. It was not something her mom and dad would be happy about, especially now. I could picture their faces. They would be disappointed and worried.

"Well, we've been talking about heroes, right?" Ms. Kramer said. "And heroes often face obstacles, setbacks, 'tough times,' right? In fact, heroes often get into trouble, from Harry Potter to Alex's favorite, Luke Skywalker, or Albert Einstein, one of my heroes. He wasn't the greatest student in his early years. He even had trouble with math. But he did know a lot about hard times. He had to flee his country to escape the Nazis. He knew about living with prejudice, racism, war."

Ms. Kramer looked up at the poster of Einstein on the wall.

"He also was very wise. He said that 'In the middle of difficulty lies opportunity'."

I looked at the poster of the old man with frizzy white hair hanging on the side of the classroom. He looked weird.

"My grandma said 'every dark cloud has a silver lining'." I remembered Grandma smiling at me when she said it. "'The trick,' Grandma said, 'was to find the lining. Don't get stuck in the dark cloud'."

"I started reading your report on your grandmother," Ms. Kramer said. "I wish I could have met her."

There was a knock on the door.

"Come in," Ms. Kramer said.

It was David.

"I found this," he said holding up the fake snake Connor had used. He dangled it from his hand and let it swing a little as he walked toward the girls, so that it looked like it was alive. Crystal jumped back. David smiled and twisted the snake in a knot, so she could see it was just rubber.

"Where'd you find it?" I asked.

"Oh, I followed Chad and Connor out of school today. I noticed they stopped by the garbage dumpsters behind the gym. I peeked in," David said. "Thought it might help."

Crystal gingerly touched the snake's tail. She gave David a quick kiss on the cheek then quickly backed away, looking down, suddenly shy.

"Well, you'd still have a hard time proving this to Mr. Fricter," Ms. Kramer said, "but this detention is over."

"Totally awesome," I said as I followed my friends out the door. The sun was shining when we stepped out of school. Little yellow flowers were starting to bloom by the school's front steps.

75

I took a deep breath and tasted the sweetness in the air. It was a perfect spring day. *Maybe you can find silver linings in dark clouds.*

Note

1 Sedgwick, W. (July, 1888). *Studies From the Biological Laboratory.* Baltimore, MD: N. Murray, Johns Hopkins University.

CHAPTER 12
Rats and cats

The frog stayed with the class for two weeks, occasionally interrupting Ms. Kramer with a 'Ribit' or a croak. She didn't seem to mind. I wondered out loud what the frog could be saying to all of us in frog language. Cami said the frog spoke in 'Frogish,' a secret frog language. Ms. Kramer asked students to translate croaks during the week.

After two weeks, the frog was gone. In its place, I saw a large cart covered by a blanket. Ms. Kramer pulled off the blanket and the class could see a cage.

"This cage is a home for little white rats. I'd like everyone to come up one at a time and take a close look at these young rats. Please watch very quietly and see what you can learn."

The students walked over to the cage and peaked in. Five little white rats ran around, sniffed, and climbed on the roof of a small house in the center of the cage. They ran on a metal wheel, spinning it around and around. Every now and then, the little rats peeked out of their cage and sniffed, pressing their noses through the cage.

Later in the day, after working on a new math chapter and more vocabulary words, Ms. Kramer asked the class what they had learned so far from watching the little rats.

"They're cute," Aliesha said.

"I hate rats," another girl said. "They're just like mice. Only they get bigger. Disgusting!"

"Rats carry diseases," Theresa said. "Ticks and germs."

"I like the way they run around," Cami said. "It looks like they're playing."

"And how do you think playing helps little rats?" Ms. Kramer asked.

"Maybe they're trying to figure things out," David said.

"And learning to climb, and jump, and run fast," Crystal said. "That would help if they had to escape real fast, like if a cat came."

"So," Ms. Kramer said, nodding her head and looking very serious, "what do you think would happen if one morning, the little rats found a cat hair, just one cat hair, in their little house? What do you think they would do?"

"They'd scream, little rat screams," Theresa said.

"And look for their mother and father rats," Aliesha said.

"Run like crazy," a boy said.

"Only there's no place to go," Alex said. "They're trapped in the cage."

"Well, scientists did an experiment[1] to find out which of your very good ideas would be right," Ms. Kramer said. "And what they found out might surprise you."

"What happened?" a girl asked.

"They froze," Ms. Kramer said. "They stopped playing and they stayed still in one part of the cage."

The class was silent as the students watched and listened to the rats scampering around their cage. It was hard to imagine they would stop because of one cat hair.

"How do you think freezing in place would help them?" Ms. Kramer asked.

"Freezing makes it harder for a cat to find them," Crystal said.

"That's right," Ms. Kramer said. "So, freezing helps at least for a while. Now, I'd like each of you to freeze right where you are. Tighten up. Imagine you are a little rat and a cat may be nearby. Try to hold yourself as tight as you can for five minutes."

Ms. Kramer pulled out a stopwatch. But before even a minute had gone by, two of the boys had poked each other, and someone giggled.

"Well, those of you who moved or made a sound just gave away your position. That would make it easier for a cat to find you."

"It's hard," a girl said.

"Well, hard as it is, the little rats did it. They kept themselves mostly frozen, as long as they could, while the cat hair was there," Ms. Kramer said. She let five minutes slowly tick by. In the back of the room, I could see Mr. Fricter scribbling in his red notebook.

"Now, I have a second question for you," Ms. Kramer said. "What would happen if you took the cat hair away after 24 hours? What would the little rats do then?"

"Playtime!" a boy called out.

"Celebrate!" another boy said with a smile.

"Well, good guesses," Ms. Kramer said, "but the scientists found that the little rats didn't go back to playing after the cat hair was removed. What do you think happened?"

"They were still afraid," Crystal said. "If a cat got into the cage and left a hair once, it could do it again."

"They're stupid," a boy said. "They're just stupid, boring rats."

I saw Mr. Fricter writing again in his red notebook. He smiled with his crooked smirk. I felt a pinprick in my stomach.

"Freezing may have been the safest thing they could do. Cami said.

"Good points," Ms. Kramer said nodding. "The little rats sensed danger and knew the danger could return. And when rats or other animals, even people, are afraid and feel trapped with no escape from something big or dangerous, their minds and bodies change. When an animal or person feels like they may be killed, hurt badly, or someone they love may be killed or hurt badly, then their fears can grow bigger and bigger until their fears take over. They can't think clearly anymore. They feel the danger. They're desperate to escape but they don't know how."

"Like after a bombing," a girl said.

"Like when everyone is afraid of a disease killing people," Theresa said.

"Right," Ms. Kramer said, "Scientists have talked about this kind of terror being like an alarm bell, an alarm bell that grows louder and louder and louder until the animal or person feels like a giant alarm clock is going off. They feel it in their body. They may feel like a giant spring ready to jump any second or feel their arms or legs moving wildly. And, if no one helps them and they see no way to escape, that's when animals or people may start doing things that don't seem to make sense."

Everyone was listening very carefully now.

"You have to know how fear works to understand how the rats were trying to survive," Ms. Kramer said. "We can learn a lot from little rats. The little rats were actually very smart. They knew that the cage was no longer safe. And it was harder for a cat to see them if they stayed perfectly still."

"What else can animals do to escape when they're scared?" Ms. Kramer asked.

"Run. Run, real fast," a boy said.

"Fight back. Bite," another boy said.

"Right," Ms. Kramer nodded again. "Sometimes, animals will start running around at hyper speed, just trying to escape, or they may start hitting, kicking, trying to fight. The problem is that if the little rats are spending all their time and energy trying to escape, fighting, or freezing, then they aren't moving around and sniffing and playing the way our little rats are playing right now. They would also not be learning or eating enough to grow healthy and strong. And, since they are trapped in the cage, they may stop trying to find a way to escape.

"Some of you may have heard about Toxic Stress or PTSD, Post Traumatic Stress Disorder, with soldiers or people who have been hurt badly in a lot of ways. Everybody feels stress some time. Some stress can help us get the energy we need to do something. But stress can become toxic or traumatic when adults or children feel or believe that they, or the people they care the most about, may be hurt badly or killed and there is no escape and no one around to protect them. Their terror can grow so large that they can't keep themselves in control. They may try to run away or they may get into a lot of fights. They may try to hide or simply freeze, not knowing what to do. And, like the little rats, they may be so busy running, fighting, hiding or freezing, that they can't learn better ways to survive or the skills they will need as grown-up rats.

"What happens if the little rats are too scared to learn how to find food?" Ms. Kramer asked.

"They could starve," a girl said.

"Are you going to scare the little rats?" Theresa asked.

"No, we're going to take good care of the little rats for the rest of this week. The little rats are here as part of our Heroes Project, to help us learn how to deal with hard times. So, let's think of ourselves as scientists learning how to help scared little rats. What could help the little rats feel safe enough to play and learn again if they had been scared by a cat hair in their cage?"

81

"They need their mommy and daddy rats," Aliesha said, "to show them it's safe again to play."

"We could help them," I said. "We could pick them up and show them it's safe."

"Wouldn't the little rats be afraid of us?" Ms. Kramer asked.

"We could take care of them, feed them, give them water," Cami said. "Show them we're nice."

"And we could pick them up in pairs," Crystal said. "That way, they would never feel alone. They would always have another rat, a friend with them."

"Buddies!" Ms. Kramer said. "These are great ideas. And some of you can help me feed the little rats this week to show the rats they are safe in our classroom. What else can we do to show the rats they are safe with us?"

"Not make any loud scary noises," a boy said.

"Keep out any animals that might scare the little rats. No cats, no dogs, no big animals," Alex said.

"Make sure no one bumps the cage," a girl said.

"Feed them at the same time every day," Aliesha said. "That's what we do with our pets at home. That way, they know what to expect. They learn they can trust us to take care of them."

"All great ideas," Ms. Kramer said. "Now, imagine you had children who were as scared as the little rats who discovered the cat hair. Imagine children who were so scared they might be hurt or killed, or that someone they loved could be hurt or killed. Imagine they were so scared that they couldn't even talk. Imagine children who were so scared that they tried to hide under their beds or in a closet. What could help those boys and girls feel safe enough to play and learn again?"

"Parents who love them," a girl said.

"Someone who could show the children they could open their eyes and ears and play again," a boy said.

"It's just like the little rats," David said. "They need someone to make them feel safe again."

"If no grown-ups do it, then the kids have to do it themselves," I said with a fierce look. "They can help each other become brave enough to look and see if it is safe." I felt my face tighten up again. My mask was set.

"And the little rats can help each other, like good friends. They can figure out how to escape," Cami said looking at me.

"Excellent," Ms. Kramer said.

I noticed that Mr. Fricter was writing busily again in his red note-book.

"For next Monday, I'd like you to write another paper," Ms. Kramer said. "This time, find a story from books or movies about heroes and write about what they learned from facing their fears or terror. What did they learn that enabled them to help other people? Maybe they learned a special skill or developed a special strength. And I'd like to give you a bonus question, something for you to think about." She paused and looked at each student.

"Why do heroes in some stories wear masks, like Batman or Spiderman? How does a secret identity help when heroes face danger? You can use our school library or ask people in your family to help you answer these questions.

"Now, who would like to help me feed the little rats?" Ms. Kramer asked. I was the only one who raised their hand. Ms. Kramer had me come up and carefully put some rat food in the food holder. I moved very slowly so I wouldn't scare the little rats. Most of them moved as far away as they could when I touched the cage. One of the little rats, though, kept sniffing and watching me.

"You're just like me," I said to the rat. "I will keep you safe." Then I gently closed the cover.

I noticed that Mr. Fricter seemed to be checking the clock every minute now. And when Ms. Kramer asked the class to pull out their vocabulary lesson, he wrote another note.

I started looking up definitions for that week's list of words. I got through 'trauma,' 'grief,' 'recovery', and 'resilience.' Then, I started imagining myself helping Mom feel better. I could help Mom, just like I helped the little rats. I just knew it.

Note

1 Panksepp, J. (1998). *Affective neuroscience: the foundations of human and animal emotions*. New York: Oxford University Press.

CHAPTER 13
Tough times

I ran into my house after school expecting to see Kevin playing with Mom. The house was quiet, way too quiet.

"Mom," I said. "Mom, Mom!"

I looked in the kitchen, then the living room, then I ran up the stairs. Kevin's door was open but he wasn't there. I peeked into Mom's bedroom. She was lying on her bed looking at the ceiling.

"Tough day," Mom said. "Tough day ..."

"Mom?" I felt my shoulders sag and my head go down. My stomach churned. I wondered what I had done this time that got Mom so worn down.

"Just go get your brother," Mom said. "And, shut the door when you leave. I need to rest."

"What?" I asked. I started to shake. My stomach really hurt now. Mom had never asked me to get Kevin by myself. I couldn't move. My feet felt like they were glued to the floor.

"Just go! I can't talk about it now."

"But, Mom ..." I stepped toward Mom's bed.

"Go! Just go! Can't you just listen to me for once in your life!"

I saw hard lines form on Mom's face. Then she rolled over on her side and all I saw was her back.

"Just go, Carrie," Mom whispered.

It was like the last weekend had never happened. 'Mean Mom' was back, the 'new mom' I didn't know and didn't want to know. I turned, ran out of the room and down the stairs. I grabbed my coat and slammed the front door behind me. This was the mom I hated.

"I'm out of here," I said out loud. It was so unfair. *How could Mom be so mean? And, now I had to take care of Kevin. … This wasn't fair. … This was. …* I looked up and saw I was almost at Kevin's school. It was twelve blocks to Kevin's school. But I had hardly even noticed the houses and cars I had passed along the way.

I yanked the front door open and marched in. The first thing I saw was a large banner over the front hall that read *Listen and Learn to Achieve* in large letters and then in smaller print just below, *Bartonsville Preschool is a proud member of the Bartonsville School District Early Education Program.*

Yuchh. There's probably a Ms. Fricter and she works here.

I walked right past the front office, not bothering to ask permission. I just peeked into rooms until I found Kevin's classroom and then opened the door. The children were sitting in a circle on the floor, listening to their teacher read a story. The teacher put her finger to her lips, without even looking up at me. She just continued her story as if I wasn't there. Boys and girls sat listening, not saying a word.

"The End," the teacher said. "Okay, play quietly until your parents come to get you."

"I'm here for my brother, Kevin," I said loudly with an edge in my voice, too loudly I knew, but I was mad about everything. I didn't care.

"Yes, your mother called and said you'd be coming. How old are you?" the teacher asked in a not very friendly voice.

"Eleven," I said and glared at the teacher. She shook her head and frowned.

I helped Kevin get his little backpack, made sure his lunch bag was inside, and put on his coat. Then, I grabbed his hand and started walking out of the school. I kept pulling Kevin's hand all the way down the street.

"You're going too fast," Kevin whined. "You're hurting my hand."

"Hurry up," I said. I realized I could be mean too, as mean as Mom. I kept on yanking Kevin as fast as I could make him go.

I saw David tossing a baseball up and down as I passed his house but I looked straight ahead.

"What up?" David asked.

I just ignored him.

"Hey, what's going on?"

"Can't you see I'm busy?"

"With what?"

"Open your eyes. My brother. My obnoxious, little brat brother. I'm taking care of him again!"

Kevin looked up at me, a sad look on his face. He whimpered. I felt bad for what I said but I was too mad to let myself care.

David looked at Kevin. "He doesn't look so awful."

"Right, like you'd ever know," I said, frowning now, just like Kevin's teacher had frowned at me. It really bothered me to see David standing there acting all calm and cool, tossing a baseball up and down, when I felt so angry inside, like I was about to explode. I was a volcano about to erupt. "Have *you ever* had to babysit in your *whole* life? Have *you* ever had to make lunch and dinner and clean up smashed strawberries, broken dishes and bloody pieces of glass?"

I knew I was becoming really mean now but I didn't care. I was so mad. I glared one more time at David. He didn't say anything so I did. "If you like my brother so much, why don't *you* ask your grandparents if they'll take him? They seem to like kids so much they took *you*!" Then, I yanked open my front door, dragged Kevin inside, and slammed the door shut.

"Go play!" I said to Kevin. Then I ran upstairs, threw myself on my bed and buried my head in my pillow. It was turning into a really rotten day.

For dinner, Mom made macaroni and cheese from a box, not the homemade kind I loved.

"That's going to be too expensive now," Mom said. "Good cheese costs a lot." She sighed. "So do fresh vegetables. And, I don't have time to cook anyway." She gave Kevin and me a few pieces of microwaved frozen green beans and carrots. My carrots still felt cold inside.

"Yuchh," I started to say, but I saw Mom looking at me. Hard lines framed Mom's face and her lips were pursed. My stomach started to ache. I felt my own face tighten up all over. I had almost forgot to put on my mask.

"I lost my job," Mom said suddenly. "Company's closing. We're going to have to tighten our belts until I find a new job." Then she looked down at her plate and picked up a forkful of macaroni, shaking her head slowly. Her eyes were moist and red.

I wondered if she had been crying all afternoon but I didn't dare ask. I hated Mom and I wished I could hug her and stop her tears all at the same time. I wanted to run away, far away, but I felt so stuck. I couldn't even get out of my chair. I just sat there with my legs kicking wildly and stared at my cold carrots and green beans.

Kevin gobbled up his macaroni like he was living in another world. Then he asked for dessert.

"No dessert," Mom whispered, shaking her head. Then, she got up from her chair and went upstairs. I heard the door close to Mom's bedroom.

"It's okay," I said softly to Kevin. "It's okay," I said again to myself as pinpricks in my stomach grew into a giant bellyache. *It has to be okay.* Then I started cleaning up the kitchen.

That night, I tossed and turned in my bed. I couldn't get to sleep. I kept seeing the hard lines form and re-form on Mom's face. Mom looked older and older every day. I imagined her shriveling up into a scary witch and I kept hearing Mom's voice cry out with a sharp edge, telling me to "Just go!"

I shuddered. I made myself think about school and remembered Ms. Kramer talking about heroes going through hard times and how everyone felt afraid sometimes, even heroes. Some people gave up. Some ran away. Heroes kept trying. Sometimes they gave up but then they came back. They learned ways to make it through the hard times, even after they got knocked down, even if they got knocked down over and over. And each time they got knocked down, they picked themselves up and became smarter and more determined. Ms. Kramer pointed to the poster of Einstein. Einstein said that "There is only one road to human greatness; the school of hard knocks." Everyone gets knocked down some time. Heroes get back up. And, each time they get themselves back up, they become stronger.

"Think about trying to cross a lake on a little boat and suddenly the wind comes up and the waves get high. Who's ever paddled a canoe?" Ms. Kramer asked the class one day.

My hand shot up along with a half dozen other students.

"A canoe can tip easily," Ms. Kramer said. "But it can also go very fast and get you across the lake. You just have to know the trick to staying balanced. How do you do stay balanced?"

"When you get into a canoe, especially on a windy day, you need to stay low in the center of the boat," I said. "If you start to lean too far on one side, you'll tip. Then you might try to balance by quickly leaning way over to the other side. If you do that, the canoe starts going over towards the other side. You can tip over, especially if the wind starts up and the waves get high. The trick is to stay in the center."

"It's the same way with feelings," Ms. Kramer said, "like being scared, sad or mad. Feelings are like the waves on a lake when a big motorboat goes by or the wind picks up. Waves may knock against the side of your canoe. It helps to calm yourself down and think about what you can do. Each wave comes and then it fades away, just like our thoughts and feelings. But, if you jerk yourself away from what you fear, you can find yourself rocking from side to side trying to escape one fear after another. And, the more you rock, the more scared you get."

Mrs. Kramer told the class to watch the people they admired and see what they do when things get hard. "What have they learned to do? How do they stay centered in their lives, just like we can center ourselves in a canoe gliding across a windy lake? How do they stay calm enough to figure out what to do when hard times come? How do they keep themselves from tipping over when things get tough?"

I felt my mind drift off. I remembered sitting in a canoe between Mom and Dad. It was back in the good days, before things got so bad. Mom and Dad would fill a cooler with picnic food. They paddled our canoe out of a small stream into a bright blue lake dotted with islands. The sun shone down and the water sparkled. A warm breeze tickled my face as I watched the water rush by the side of the canoe my parents had rented. Mom paddled in the bow. I sat in the center and Dad paddled behind me. I remembered how a large motorboat came rushing by pulling a water skier behind. Large waves from the motorboat headed for our canoe. The waves looked higher than the sides of the canoe. I looked back at my dad.

"It's best to hit the waves head on," Dad said. He ruddered the canoe. Then, Dad and Mom paddled us hard, head on into the waves. "Now, the waves can't tip us," Dad said. "We can sit back and enjoy the bumps like a little roller coaster in the middle of the lake." And that's what we did. I threw up my hands after the canoe hit the first bump, just like I did when Mom, Dad, and I went on a roller coaster. I laughed as we went up and down, flying a little way into the air with each bump. A light spray of warm lake water splashed my face. I remembered how my cheeks tingled. Then the lake became calm and peaceful again. The breeze stopped and the water looked like a mirror. I looked back and saw Dad smiling. I heard Mom in front of me softly singing an old song.

I felt myself start to smile as I remembered my family canoeing, but I quickly tightened my face. I didn't want to think too much about Mom and Dad and I knew my answer to Ms. Kramer's question. I knew what to do when the waves came. *Stay low. Stay centered. Turn your canoe into the waves. Hit the waves head on. Hit the waves hard.* Ride the waves up and down. And, I knew that was just what I was going to do.

CHAPTER 14
Friends forever

I was eager to get to school the next day, even glad to work on arithmetic and vocabulary all morning. It was good to be busy.

The class went to gym which was actually fun that day, probably because Chad and Connor were gone. I had seen Chad's mother pick them up and take them somewhere. After gym, our class went right to lunch and afterwards to a special program in the gym about getting ready for middle school. Chairs had been set up in the gym and the principal and teachers from the middle school spoke from the stage at the end of the gym. It was a little boring but 'whatever.' At least we'd be leaving Bartonsville Elementary.

When we got back to the classroom, I could feel that something was wrong. There was just something in the air, something bad, but I didn't know what. My stomach twinged, just a little. Then, Aliesha cried out, "A little rat is missing. It's gone!"

"Where?" Theresa asked.

"There were five, right?" Aliesha said. "Now there are just four."

"He could be anywhere!" Theresa shrieked.

"Maybe a cat came and ate him," Chad snickered.

Theresa screamed again.

"What's going on here?" Mr. Fricter asked. "Into your seats." Then, he turned towards Ms. Kramer. His eyes seemed strangely bright and the left side of his mouth curled up just a little more than usual.

"I'll have to report this."

He walked by my desk as he left the class. I felt an urge to trip him as he went by. I almost did it too.

"We'll find our little fellow," Ms. Kramer said to the class. "Remember, little rats are rather hardy and very smart. And they won't bother any of you. Right now, let's turn to Social Studies. And, while you're working on your chapter questions, I will look around the classroom."

But the class didn't get very far before they were interrupted by Principal Pratt who pulled Ms. Kramer out into the hall for a few minutes. Mr. Fricter walked up to the front of the classroom and smiled his crooked smile, making sure he looked at every one of the students.

"We're moving to the gym to finish today's class," Ms. Kramer said when she returned to the classroom.

The rest of the day seemed to drag on forever. After I got home from school, Mom called and said she'd be late. She was interviewing for jobs. She arranged for Tammy, a 16-year-old girl who lived across the street, to babysit. Mom asked me to go with Tammy to get Kevin from his Preschool. I knew what that really meant. I would play with Kevin while Tammy spent the whole time texting her friends. When Mom returned, we had leftover meatballs and spaghetti for dinner. After dinner, Mom told me to dust and vacuum the upstairs bedrooms and hallway.

"Tomorrow, we'll clean the downstairs," Mom said.

The next day was even worse.

The class spent all Wednesday in the gym. Ms. Kramer kept being called on the loudspeaker to go to Principal Pratt's office. That meant a lot of the day was spent doing paperwork with Mr. Fricter walking up and down between the old desks the janitor had pulled out from somewhere. Mr. Fricter hummed to himself as he checked the students' work. He seemed rather happy. I thought about tripping him again.

My back hurt from the disgusting desk. And, later that night at home, Mom yelled at me at least five times for not paying attention while I was dusting the furniture.

"This house is a mess," Mom kept saying.

Meanwhile, I was thinking, who cares about dust on the furniture? My whole life was messed up. Upstairs, I could hear Kevin running around, playing with his action figures, shooting at each other.

"If he goes in my room, I'll kill him," I said out loud.

"Carrie, what did you say?"

I didn't say anything.

"Get the moldings too, like I showed you," Mom said.

I kicked the couch.

"What was that?"

"Nothing."

That night, I thrashed from side to side in my bed. I couldn't get to sleep. When my alarm clock went off, I felt half-asleep. On the school bus that morning, Chad and Connor were snickering away. I felt my fists tighten. My legs were swinging wildly again, like they were kicking at imaginary monsters. I wanted to kick Chad and Connor, kick them hard. I imagined kicking the smirks off their faces. Cami sat down next to me on the bus. She kept trying to make little jokes, but I just sat there, kicking my legs. My lips were pressed tight. Tight cheeks, tight eyes, my mask was in place. No one could see what I really felt inside.

All of the Class 5D students went right to the gym, just like we had done the day before. But, today, neither Ms. Kramer nor Mr. Fricter was there. Instead, Principal Pratt stood in front of the makeshift rows of desks.

"You can go back to your classroom, today," she said. "The janitor has looked everywhere in the classroom. It's perfectly safe to go back. Wherever the little rat went, he's not in the classroom. Mr. Fricter is back in the classroom waiting for you now. I wasn't able to get a substitute teacher so Mr. Fricter will lead the class for the next few days."

"Where's Ms. Kramer?" I asked. I didn't want to spend another minute with Mr. Fricter and his crooked smirk.

"She's on temporary leave," Principal Pratt said.

"What does that mean?" Aliesha asked.

"She's been fired!" Connor called out, laughing. Chad snickered but most of the students looked stunned.

"The President of the School Board has asked the Superintendent to look into our fifth-grade program and what happened in Classroom 5D," Principal Pratt said.

"Look into what?" I asked.

"Concerns from parents. Concerns from a staff member. And, now, safety concerns over a missing rat. Some parents are worried the rat could have spread diseases. I can't really say any more."

"Those little rats were perfectly healthy," I said.

"Oh, right. And you're a rat expert!" Chad said grinning. I wanted to kick him, hard.

"Takes a rat to know one," Connor said. Then he smiled at Chad.

'Boo yah!"

"Quiet," Principal Pratt said. "The school board is having a meeting next Wednesday to discuss the fifth-grade curriculum at Bartonsville Elementary. I will be looking into what happened. Then, I will determine whether Ms. Kramer will return to your class. And if so, what she will be teaching. In the meantime, Mr. Fricter will be in charge."

"No!" Crystal cried out.

Cami, David, and I groaned, so did several other students.

"I'll be coming in the classroom as much as I can to help lead the class," Principal Pratt said. "That will give me a good chance to get to know you. Right now, it's time to pick up your books and anything else you've put in these desks. Then line up."

David, Cami, Crystal, and I were the last to line up. I turned to my friends as the rest of the class started to move forward.

"We've got to do something for Ms. Kramer."

"Have you seen how Chad and Connor have been smiling and laughing so much lately?" Crystal asked.

"Every day since the little rat was lost, from the minute they get on the bus," I said.

"I heard them talking at lunch," Cami said. "Their parents have been writing letters to the school board president and the superintendent. They've been complaining about Ms. Kramer, saying she was wasting class time and not helping students get ready for the fifth-grade state exams. And then, she endangered the class by bringing rats into the classroom and letting one escape."

"Mr. Fricter looked pretty happy too," I said. "I bet he's the 'staff member' who complained."

"He's probably still mad that we got out of detention early," Crystal said. "And I heard Theresa say her parents were upset about Ms. Kramer talking about animals dying in class. What's that about?"

"Probably the story of the frog experiment, where the frog could have died in the hot water," Cami said.

"What can we do?" Crystal asked.

"We could start by finding the little rat," David said.

"How are we going to do that?" Crystal asked.

"I've seen where Chad and Connor dump things," David said. "In one of the dumpsters, behind the gym. The same place they put the snake. They've also tossed other stuff in there. If they took the little rat, they might have thrown him there too. He might still be there."

"Hopefully alive," Cami said. A sad look came over her face. "You don't think they killed the little rat?"

"Gross," Crystal said. "Why would they kill a cute little rat?"

"Move along, back there," Principal Pratt said from the front of the line as the students walked back to their classroom.

"We'd better look as soon as we can, before they come to empty the garbage," I said. Then I remembered, "Oh, no. No! I can't do it today. My mother asked me to go right home. She couldn't get a babysitter. I have to catch the bus and go get Kevin from his school."

"I can search for the little rat," Cami said, a determined look on her face. She looked at Crystal.

"Me too," Crystal said nodding. "But I don't want to touch it."

"Okay," David said. "Wait 'til Chad and Connor leave, then meet me in the back."

Four sets of hands shot out.

"Fist-bump power-tower," Crystal said. We made an eight-fisted tower, one fist on top of another. We were like a champion soccer team in the playoffs, trailing by one point with thirty seconds remaining. The stakes were high. We had a plan. We had each other. We were ready to score.

"Friends forever," I said. Then Cami and Crystal joined in, "Stick together!"

CHAPTER 15

Grandma's double-rich, dangerously deep-dark chocolate brownies

Mr. Fricter stood in the front of the classroom when the children returned. He was smiling his crooked half-smile. The rat cage was gone.

"Thank you, Principal Pratt," he said graciously with a so very gentle voice. "We will begin today with math. Students, please open your books to page 128."

Principal Pratt stood in the back of the classroom for about 20 minutes as Mr. Fricter read from our math book. It was boring beyond belief.

Mr. Fricter's lecture was interrupted by the school secretary on the intercom asking Principal Pratt to come back to her office. Mr. Fricter's crooked smile got a little bigger as Principal Pratt left the room.

"Thank you, students, for your excellent participation and questions," he said in his gentle voice, even though none of the students had said a word. Then, his lips curled down and his voice returned to his normal growl. "Discussion's over. Time to work. Answer the questions on pages 181 to 189."

The rest of the day was pretty much the same with Principal Pratt returning, watching from the back of the classroom then leaving whenever she was called back to her office. After lunch, Mr. Fricter had the students take turns reading out loud from their social studies textbook. Then he assigned more questions to be answered and sat down at the teacher's desk, smiling his crooked smile.

After a couple minutes, Chad walked up to Mr. Fricter, a sad look pasted on his face. I noticed that Connor stood up and walked towards the teacher's desk as if he was also going to ask for help with the assignment. On his way, Connor shoved his social studies textbook hard into David's back. The blow almost knocked David out of his seat and sent David's social studies book and papers shooting forward. His book hit Theresa's back.

"Hey!" David yelled.

Then Theresa screamed, "Ouch! That hurt! That really hurt!"

Mr. Fricter jumped up and marched over to Theresa's desk. He picked up the social studies book that had landed behind her on the floor.

"David," he read solemnly from the book's inside jacket. "You lost your social studies book. Looks like you need some extra help learning how to be appropriately *social*. After school, today, in detention, and it won't be a short one."

Mr. Fricter returned to the teacher's desk where two eager students, Chad and Connor, waited patiently for his help, their faces looking like little angels.

I didn't know what to do. My legs started jerking back and forth wildly. The bell finally rang after what I thought was the longest day I had ever had in school. The end of school didn't make me feel any better though. I felt my heart sink into my stomach as I left my friends. I forced myself to walk out the door and get on the bus before it left.

I slumped down in a seat by myself. Chad and Connor got on the bus, grinning and laughing. I could hear them snickering and snorting. By the time the bus got to my stop, I felt worn down. My shoulders sagged under my backpack as I trudged over to Kevin's preschool. I felt like I was carrying a hundred thousand pounds.

I walked under the *Listen and Learn* banner and followed the sounds of the children out to the backyard. Kevin was chanting

'Ring around the Rosie' with two boys and a girl. They did it in 'little kid' voices but in a strange way, it sounded more like a march than a fun song to sing. When they got to 'All fall down,' each of them collapsed on the grass, lay there for a few seconds, and then slowly stood back up. None of them smiled.

"Well done," a teacher standing near the children said, a serious look on her face. But I knew there was something missing. Where was the laughter? Where was the rhyming song I had loved as a little girl? I remembered jumping up with my friends after we fell down, holding each other's hands, and running as fast as we could round and round, pulling ourselves outwards until we crashed down once more. Then we would laugh and jump right back up, happy and strong.

"Line up," the teacher said. "Tallest first. Shortest last."

One of the boys bumped into another boy ahead of him who pushed him back.

"I'm taller," the boy in front said.

"Stay in line!" the teacher said. "Listen to what I say. Keep your hands to yourselves. Walk. Don't talk."

I grabbed Kevin's hand.

"We're getting out of here," I said.

As soon as we got home, I called Cami's house.

Cami's mother answered, "No, Cami isn't back yet. I'll have her call you when she gets in."

I paced up and down the upstairs hall, checking every few minutes out my bedroom window to see if David had come home. Every minute seemed like an hour. Finally, the phone rang. It was Cami. She told me she and Crystal searched two of the three dumpsters, she said. Then a teacher spotted them and told them to go home. Cami said they would try again the next day.

My head slumped and my stomach ached. At least, I'd be able to help tomorrow. I just hoped it would not be too late.

I peeked into Kevin's bedroom and watched him play with his action figures. I didn't really know the names of Kevin's super-heroes. And I usually didn't care. I watched as Kevin had a large, powerful action figure tell other figures: "Walk. Don't talk. Don't ask questions. Just do what I say!" Then the large figure whacked the smaller figure on the head.

I wondered where Kevin learned to play like that. I went back to pacing the hall. A few minutes later, I peeked into Kevin's room again. I saw him open his bottom dresser drawer and pull some old shirts away. Then, he pulled out a bag and opened it up. I saw something brown inside.

"What's that?" I asked from the doorway.

"Nothing," Kevin said and quickly stuffed the bag into his drawer. He slammed the drawer shut. Then, he sat down in front of the dresser, looking at his hands. He was shaking.

"Kevin, show me."

"No."

"I have to see if it's safe."

Kevin looked up at me and started to cry.

"Don't tell Mom. Don't tell."

I put my hands on Kevin's shoulders and shook my head. Then I opened the drawer and reached into the bag. I pulled out two crumbled brownies that I remembered from the week before and something else that looked mushy and yellowish-white. White fuzzy stuff was growing all over it.

"Apple pie," I said picking up the bag.

Kevin grabbed on to my leg.

"Give it to me! Give it to me."

"I don't want you to get sick. Old food can make you sick. It's spoiled." Kevin clung to my leg crying.

"Let go and follow me," I said. "I'll find you something good to eat."

I walked into the kitchen and started looking through the cabinets. I didn't see anything ready to eat.

"I know!" I said, "Yumm, that sounds good to me. Yum for the tum!" I started getting the pans out, humming as I opened cabinets.

"You know what, Kevin. We're going to do some baking. You and me, like the old days."

I pulled down Mom's recipe book and thumbed through the well-worn pages.

"Here it is! *Grandma's Double-Rich Dangerously Deep-Dark Chocolate Brownies*. What do you think?"

Kevin looked up at me. Tears were rolling down his face.

"I taste the chocolate," he said and he started to smile.

CHAPTER 16
Broken glass

It was Thursday lunchtime after the most boring Fricter class ever. Cami and I picked up hot vegetable soup and meatless spaghetti in the cafeteria and headed for our favorite table. At least it smelled good, I thought, carrying my tray.

Just as we were about to sit down, Chad and Connor came up behind Cami. Chad rammed her from behind with the corner of his tray. Cami fell forward. Her soup, her plate of spaghetti and a glass of milk crashed onto the floor. I heard the glass shatter and saw jagged pieces of glass shoot out in all directions. Red soup and spaghetti sauce were splattered all over the floor. Worse, Cami fell onto the broken glass.

"Aww," Cami cried out. I could see red glass shards stuck into her arm.

"Whoops. Oh dear. 'So sorry'," Chad said with a big smile and a fake accent mocking Chinese-Americans.

"___ off!" I yelled.

"Oooh! You're so bad! I'm really scared!" Chad said.

Connor stepped behind me. "Hey, miss your little rat friends?" he asked smiling.

Chad grinned and moved in front of me. "Yah, I bet they remind you of your family. Maybe yo' mama?"

Suddenly, I felt Connor's tray jab me hard in my lower back knocking me forward. Somehow, I held on to my tray. I felt a sharp stabbing pain in my back.

"Oh, I'm so …" Connor started to say in his fake sad voice. But before he could finish, I whirled around, lifted my tray and slammed it into Connor's face.

"Awwwwwwwww!" Connor screamed as hot soup dribbled off his face. Red streaks flowed down his face on to his shirt with chunks of vegetables. Red blobs of spaghetti clung to his shirt.

"You burned me," Connor cried out, his voice throbbing. "Are you nuts? You're whacko!"

A cafeteria aide came running up.

"What happened here?" she asked.

"I saw it all. That nut job shoved her tray into Connor," Chad said, pointing at me, "She's nuts. She's really …"

But before he could finish, I hit him hard, just below his eye. Chad fell back. Then, I kicked him hard in the leg. Chad stumbled and howled. I kicked him again and again, as hard as I could. I kept on kicking.

"Stop it," a school resource officer yelled, running over. He was a large man with broad shoulders and coal black hair.

Chad charged towards me. I raised my fists and glared at him. The cafeteria aide grabbed my arms from behind. I saw Chad lurching forward to slug me. I started kicking wildly and broke free from the cafeteria aide.

"I said 'stop.' I mean stop!" the resource officer bellowed. He grabbed me around my waist. I swiveled and kicked him hard. I jumped to the side as he tried to grab me and I kicked him again. The officer shoved me down slamming my face onto the floor. It hurt but I didn't care. I could see Chad circling around, his fists raised, a menacing look in his eyes. I kicked backwards and struck the officer hard. For a second, I felt like I could get away. I rolled over.

"Stay down," the officer commanded. He was over me now, holding my arms down.

The cafeteria aide grabbed my feet. I struggled to get free, trying to kick the aide. Together, the officer and the cafeteria aide picked me up and carried me out of the cafeteria. I was thrashing wildly in the air, kicking as hard as I could.

"Whack job!" Connor yelled.

The officer and the cafeteria aide carried me to a room next to the principal's office. I just kept kicking and kicking. A police officer arrived and slapped handcuffs on me. He had trouble putting them on, probably because my arms are so skinny and I kept on kicking at him. The officer tightened the handcuffs. The cold metal cut into my wrists. I was too mad to cry. Instead, I screamed at him with every swear word I knew.

After some time, Principal Pratt came in and gave me a choice of waiting quietly for my mother to come or being taken to the police station. I was worn out by then and just glared at her. She asked me again.

"Stay here," I mumbled. I almost spit at her. I kicked the chair one more time then sat down.

I spent the next hour and a half waiting in a room next to the principal's office. The police officer took off the handcuffs after about an hour and stood outside the door. I had red marks on my wrists. My clothes were stained with soup and spaghetti sauce. My face stung. My wrists ached. My throat hurt from screaming. I didn't care.

My mother arrived and walked into Principal Pratt's office. I put my head down. I didn't want to see Mom's face. I didn't want to see anyone.

"What did you do?" Mom asked after talking to Principal Pratt.

I pressed my chin hard into my chest and stared at the floor.

"Tell me what happened," Mom said. I pulled my sweater over my head.

"I don't know what's the matter with you. *Suspended.* Just what I need now, after everything else!"

I stared at the floor through my sweater. I heard a big sigh, and then a loud sniffle like Mom was gasping for air.

"Do you realize this will cost me a new job? Do you know what that means? I had to leave a job interview to come get you. If I didn't come to school, they said they were taking you to the police station. The police, Carrie! The resource officer said you kicked him and a cafeteria aide. They might press charges. Some boy said his parents are going to sue us because you burned him."

I heard Mom sigh again.

"People are getting laid off all over town. Now this!"

I could picture Mom's face full of hard lines, the words coming out like little knives from her hard-pressed lips. I wanted to yell back, *It was better with Dad! He tried to get us out of this stink-hole town!* But I kept my lips sealed tight. Nothing came out.

I heard Mom stand up. I felt my neck and face get hot. I knew Mom was staring down at me. Hot tears grew in my eyes but I wasn't going to let myself cry. *Not ever.* And I wasn't going to say anything, nothing at all. I just stared at the floor so hard I could have burned holes in the tiles.

"Get your backpack. Let's go!" Mom said.

I followed Mom out to the car. It was Grandma's old car that Mom started driving after Grandma died. My parents had said it was better than Mom's old car. Another lie! I climbed in then slammed the car door and stared out the side window.

Mom started to drive the car out of the school parking lot, then jerked the car to a stop. I felt Mom's eyes burning into my neck again.

"Look at me," Mom said. "Look at me, Carrie."

I turned my head towards her. It was okay to face her now. I had my mask back on. I just stared at my mother. She couldn't see what I was thinking inside. She couldn't see the volcano about to erupt. And she couldn't see the fire under the volcano, and under the fire, the gut ache, and under the gut ache, how scared I was. Mom stared at me and then sadly shook her head. We rode the rest of the way home without a word, just silence, not even the radio.

"What got into you?" Mom asked again at dinner.

"Nothing," I said. My lips were pressed so tight hardly a sound came out. Mom didn't ask again.

I cleaned up the dishes then went up to my room. The phone rang and I heard Mom tell someone that I couldn't answer any calls. Whoever called would have to call back.

I couldn't sleep much that night. And when I did, I dreamed of glass breaking with sharp, jagged shards scattered all around. Some were soaked red with blood. Some sparkled. Loud voices were screaming.

"I'm not moving. I said 'No'! I mean 'No!'"

"You're nuts. You know it, nuts!"

"Get out! Just go. Get out!"

Then I heard the sound of breaking glass. I jumped out of bed and started running for the stairway, crying out "Stop! Stop!"

I woke up when I got to the top of the stairs and slowly trudged back to my room. The night weighed down on me with darkness and gloom. My stomach ached as if I had swallowed the broken glass in my dreams.

I kept on dreaming of broken glass and jumping up from my bed until the early morning light drove away the darkness. And then I remembered. I was just too tired to fight it off anymore. It was the worst time ever, the time I never wanted to remember, the terrible time I thought I had locked away forever. But it all came flooding back to me, unstoppable, like the light streaming into my room.

It was the last fight.

I had heard Mom and Dad arguing downstairs. I couldn't sleep with them yelling at each other. I just kept tossing and turning and trying to cover my ears, but I wasn't able to get my parents' yelling out of my head. I kept thinking "Why can't they just get along? Why can't we be a normal family."

"I can get a better job if we move," Dad was saying, "then we wouldn't be in such a mess."

"I don't want to move. I've told *you*," Mom said. "This is my mother's home. This is *my* home. This is where I grew up. This is my town. You obviously don't care what happens here. If you want to move, go ahead. Go. Leave me! Leave the kids!"

"I want you to move with me. And the kids!"

"Just go! I can't talk about this!"

It was the same old argument, the same old stuff since my dad lost his job. At first, I heard my parents argue just once in a while. But then it seemed like every week and then almost every night. And each night the arguments had become a little louder, a little angrier, a little longer. I imagined their angry words flying through the air like knives, first little knives and then big knives. And, every night, I felt my heart beat a little faster, a little louder. Knots grew in my stomach and turned into pinpricks.

I closed my eyes tight and tried to tune my parents out but I couldn't stop hearing them bickering. Louder, then quiet, then more arguing.

I wanted to tell them to stop. *Just get along. Be nice to each other. Do what you tell Kevin and me to do!*

After a while, their voices usually died down and then I would let myself drift off to sleep. Before they stopped, I would lie in bed, tossing and turning, trying to think of something I could say or do. But I couldn't think of anything. Nothing. At least, I had told myself, if I stay up, I will know the argument is over. I will know if I need to do something. So that was what I did. Sometimes for a few minutes. Sometimes, for what seemed like hours. I'd finally fall asleep when it got quiet.

Except one night. That was the night I failed to stay awake. I fell asleep before my parents stopped arguing. Some time later, I jumped up from a deep sleep and heard the yelling still going on. I thought at first I was having another nightmare.

"What do you care? You're leaving," Mom yelled.

"We can't pay the bank," Dad answered.

"If you worked a little harder.... If you made sure you got paid once in a while ..." Mom sounded bitter, mad. "Maybe you could eat less at restaurants and cook for a change."

"You're going to lose the house," Dad's voice was steady but cold with an angry edge. "Your Mom's house."

I heard Mom scream something and then a crash. I ran to the stairs and almost fell halfway down, stumbling in the dark. I ran into the kitchen. Dad was standing by the wall, behind the kitchen table. His eyes were wide and his lips were pressed together tight in a line. A little blood trickled down his arm, dripping on to the floor. Around his feet, I saw shards of glass. There was a dent in the wall, inches from where Dad stood.

"I can't take this anymore!" Dad said glaring at Mom.

I turned and saw Mom standing behind the kitchen counter. Her face was clenched tight. Her eyes were like little dots. Her lips were curled down. She looked so mad, for a second I thought Mom's head might explode. Mom opened her mouth as if she was about to swear. I knew that look. My heart started pounding.

Suddenly Mom stopped. She turned her head and her eyes widened. I felt my heart freeze. Mom stared at me. She pursed her lips tight.

I looked from Mom to Dad. I didn't know what to say. But I knew, even more, that I had to say something—something to keep Mom and Dad together, something to save our family. I felt my mouth open but I couldn't breathe.

I felt Mom's eyes drilling into my own and deeper still, beneath my eyes into my brain. I didn't know what to say. I was frozen. It was like we were all frozen. No one moved. No one said anything, not a sound. Meanwhile my parents' rage filled the kitchen and grew into what felt like a bomb that was about to explode.

Dad shook his head. Then he stared at Mom.

"That's it. Stay here. I'm moving."

I gasped. I could hardly breathe. I tried to talk. I wanted to say something, to make them stop arguing. I had to say something to keep Dad from leaving but nothing came out.

"Great. That's just like you. Do whatever you want! You come first!" Mom said.

"You could come too," Dad said in a softer voice, a sad voice.

"I said 'no'. I meant no!" Hard lines framed the sides of Mom's face. I watched Mom turn and leave the kitchen.

"Just go already!" she screamed from the living room.

I looked up at Dad.

"I didn't want you to see this," Dad said softly.

I could feel tears dripping down my face, hot and sticky. Inside, my heart beat louder and louder. Knots filled my stomach. A voice cried out from inside me, "Don't leave! You can't leave!" But nothing came out of my mouth, even when Dad walked towards me. I felt him kiss my forehead. I smelled his aftershave like an ocean breeze, the aftershave he always wore since I was a little girl. But his face was different, changed. He looked older with lines stretched down the side of his face. I saw the corners of his lips try to smile, but the smile never came. Then, he put his hands on my shoulders.

"Look after your little brother, Carrie. We'll get through this. You'll see."

But I couldn't see. Everything was a blur. Everything was spinning. Everything was wrong. I was to blame. I should never have fallen asleep. Tears covered my face. Dad gave me another kiss on my forehead. Then he turned and opened the door to the garage.

I heard the car start. I ran to the door.

"Come back. Daddy, Come back. Come back," I screamed. I saw Dad's car back out of the garage and drive away. I was too late.

I wanted to run after Dad but my legs wouldn't budge. I turned back into the kitchen and stared at the broken glass and red drops of Dad's blood on the floor.

A few minutes later, Mom came back into the kitchen. Her lips were tight.

"Go back to bed, Carrie. You've got school tomorrow."

I watched Mom take out a broom and sweep up the glass.

"Mommy ..." I said. My voice was faint, desperate.

"Just go to bed, Carrie," Mom said. "I can't talk now." She bent to pick up some of the shattered glass.

I stood frozen. I felt like I was a little girl again. Helpless.

"S___! I cut my finger," Mom screamed. She picked a jagged piece of glass out of her hand.

I could see blood running down the side of Mom's hand.

"Mommy ..." I cried out but my voice was more like a whisper. I wanted to scream but all the air had been sucked out of my lungs.

"Go to bed." Mom was staring at her bleeding hand. She stood there watching the blood drip, Mom's blood dripping on the floor mixing with the shards of glass, Mom's blood and Dad's blood.

I couldn't stop staring at Mom's blood dripping on the kitchen floor.

"Mommy," I whispered.

"Just go already!"

I turned and trudged up the stairs. My feet felt like they were weighted down with lead. My head ached and my heart throbbed. My stomach felt like it had been pricked by a hundred needles. I threw myself on my bed. I cried until I ran out of tears.

The doorbell rang. I must have fallen asleep. The clock said 4:30 AM. I stumbled out of bed. My face was still wet with tears. The doorbell rang again. I could see two police officers at the front door. I felt a tremor swell in my belly, a searing pain like my gut was screaming. *What had I done?*

I stood in the front hall frozen, speechless. I wanted to run away but I had nowhere to go. I heard footsteps come from behind. Mom opened the door.

"What is it?" Mom asked the officers.

"Mrs. Sanderson?" one of the officers asked.

Mom nodded.

"I'm terribly sorry Ma'am. Your husband was in a car crash last night. A truck ran a red light crossing the highway. Your husband swerved but the truck hit him."

"Where is he?" Mom cried out. Her eyes bulged. Her body shook.

"I'm sorry, Ma'am," the officer said. "I'm terribly sorry."

"Where is he?" Mom shrieked.

"He didn't make it," the officer said.

I ran up to my room. I slammed my door and threw myself on my bed pulling the blankets over my head. My legs started thumping, kicking wildly, up, down, out of control. I hated Dad for leaving us. I hated Mom for driving him away. I wanted to kick and kick. I wanted to kick them all. But, I couldn't. I just kept kicking the bed wildly.

That's when I vowed to lock that night away, to never remember, to never cry again. *Never ever!* That was the day I put on my mask.

I knew I should have stopped them from arguing. I should have stopped Dad from leaving. He didn't hear me or he didn't care enough to stay. Either way, I knew I had failed. I lost Dad. And I couldn't bear for anyone to see how I horrible I was. If anyone asked, I would pretend Dad was just away, working in another city. I didn't want anyone to see how I felt, even myself.

I remembered all of this as sunlight slowly entered my room driving the darkness away. It was the worst night ever. It was over a year ago but it felt like it had just happened. Now, up in my room, lying on my bed, I felt tears growing in my eyes. *Not now. Not ever!*

My body shook. I couldn't fight the sadness anymore. Hot wet tears streaked down my face. I felt myself cry and cry until I had no more tears left. Then, I just lay there breathing slowly, shuddering with each breath.

I fell asleep and when I woke up, I remembered something else. It was Ms. Kramer, touching the back of my hair, a warm look in her eyes, and then Ms. Kramer's voice, soft and soothing. I remembered Ms. Kramer telling the class,

"When something is really bad, just write it down. Put your problems on a piece of paper, the things that really bother you, even your nightmares. Turn 'tough times' into words on paper that tell the story of what happened, what you saw, heard, felt, and did. You can add pictures, if you like. Write it all down. You can put the problems away to be solved later, or you can use your story to help you share the 'tough times' with someone you really trust. That way, you won't be alone. Worries and fears become challenges you can figure out together with friends and family members, 'tough times' you share and solve instead of nightmares you have to relive by yourself."

Ms. Kramer had explained how the story could be very simple and short, just three parts, or chapters, a beginning, a middle, and an end. The *Middle* chapter would be the hard times including how it felt deep inside. The *Beginning* chapter would be how you remembered good times from before the bad time, good memories that you wanted to keep, good feelings, and good times. And the *End* chapter would be about what adults, other children and you have done to make things better and what could keep the bad times from happening again. That way, the story would be changed from being about how you were stuck in bad times into a story about how you could get *through* the bad times to better times.

"It's a story about making things better together with the people you care about and the people who care about you."

I jumped out of bed. I grabbed a pencil off my desk. Then, I wrote out the story, the story of broken glass, the story of how I had failed, the story of my broken family.

I wrote fast. My pencil almost seemed to fly across the paper. Then I folded the paper three times, put it in an envelope, licked the flap, and sealed it shut. I hid it under my socks in the top drawer of my dresser.

CHAPTER 17
Rescue

I spent all day Friday in my room. Mom called from another job interview to check on me and told me to pick Kevin up at school again. She told me I was lucky to just have a one-day suspension and that was probably only because the school was having a problem getting the video recorders in the cafeteria to replay what happened and back up what the cafeteria aide and the resource officer said.

I knew what happened but I didn't say anything. *What was the point?*

I had just walked home after getting Kevin when the doorbell rang. I ran down the stairs and saw my friends on my front steps.

"We did it!" Cami said. She had bandages all over her right arm from where she had fallen on the glass in the cafeteria but she looked okay.

Crystal had a big smile on her face.

"We found the little rat! High fives!"

I almost jumped out the door. I hugged my friends.

"How'd you find him?"

"We got caught yesterday searching the garbage cans and had to leave. But we snuck back today," Crystal said, grinning from ear to ear.

"David got detention again from Mr. Fricter so it was just the two of us. We waited by the bus until Chad and Connor got on, then we just turned around," Cami said, her eyes sparkling with excitement.

"We pretended we forgot something inside the school," Crystal said. "Then, after we got inside, we just walked out the back door to the garbage dumpsters."

"It was disgusting," Cami said, still smiling.

"But Cami was very brave," Crystal said.

"Crystal was brave too,' Cami said. "We started pulling everything out of the closest dumpster to the back door, the one where David found the fake snake. One stinky thing at a time. Yuchh! It stunk."

"Until we could see the bottom. And there he was. I ripped a milk carton in half then scooped him up," Crystal said proudly. "I thought he might be dead. But he moved his leg. He's still alive."

Cami held up a brown paper bag with a milk carton inside and small holes all around the top. "He's inside the bag," she said, a worried look on her face. "He's still lying in the milk carton."

"We've been trying to get him to eat or drink. But he hasn't moved. He's in bad shape," Crystal said.

"We've got to get him to a veterinarian," Cami said. "I think he's hurt or something. He's got blue patches on his belly. He barely moves."

"David told me his grandfather used to be a veterinarian," I said. "They live next door. Let's go." I started down the steps, then suddenly I stopped. I shook my head.

"Wait here a minute. I've got to get Kevin."

Mrs. Cohen greeted my friends, Kevin and me with a big smile.

"David's not back yet from school but you're welcome to come in and wait for him."

"I want to go home and play," Kevin said. He yanked at my arm, tugging me back towards our house but I held him firmly. I wasn't going to leave my friends. No way! Kevin kept tugging but quickly changed his mind when Mrs. Cohen brought out a plate with crackers, cheese and a bowl filled with green grapes.

A few minutes later, David came home. Dr. Cohen joined us at the kitchen table.

"What have we here?" Dr. Cohen asked in a pleasant voice.

"Hi, Papa," David said.

"We found the missing little rat," Crystal said.

The children quickly shared the story of what had happened with Dr. Cohen and how they believed Chad and Connor had taken the little rat and tossed it into the dumpster.

"I'd better have a look at the little guy," Dr. Cohen said. The four older children followed him as he carried the bag with the little rat back into the garage. Kevin stayed and played at the kitchen table with a coloring book and a set of markers David's grandmother brought out.

Dr. Cohen put the bag on top of a shiny steel table and pulled down some veterinary tools from a shelf above. He put on special gloves and opened the paper bag, carefully lifting the baby rat onto a large tray with high sides.

"Little fellow looks hurt. He's weak. Looks like he needs water too. Faded bruises on his sides. Looks like he's been squeezed, squeezed hard, by fingers, little fingers. See how the bruises are small and round."

The children looked at the little rat and saw round pale bluish red marks on both sides of the rat's belly. David's grandfather put a little bowl of water in front of the rat. The children watched as the little rat slumped by the dish. After a little while, he sniffed and then put out his tongue. Dr. Cohen gently squirted a little water into the rat's mouth with an eye dropper. The rat closed his mouth but nothing happened. They watched the little rat lie there. Just when I was about to give up, the little rat opened his mouth. His tongue moved. Dr. Cohen gave him another squirt. He slumped down. But a few minutes later, he lifted his head and sipped a little more water.

"That's a good sign," Dr. Cohen smiled. "I will take this fellow over to the Animal Hospital. I know the vet there. She's very good. They'll take good care of him. I also need to notify Principal Pratt."

"Not Principal Pratt," I said. "She suspended Ms. Kramer.'"

"She put Mr. Fricter in charge," Crystal said.

"Yes, but she's also responsible for finding out what happened and making sure all of you, and the other students, get a good education. She needs to know," Dr. Cohen said. "Keep an eye on our little rat here, while I go make some calls."

A few minutes later, David's grandfather returned.

"I'm taking your little rat to the Animal Hospital. Principal Pratt was in her office when I called. She's going to meet us there."

"She'll blame Cami and Crystal," I said. "We'll be in more trouble then. We'll probably all get suspended! My mom will kill me!"

"Mine too," Cami said.

Dr. Cohen looked at the four children, a kind look on his face.

"You can tell Principal Pratt the facts. Just tell the truth. Truth wins in the end."

"Not anymore," I said, shaking my head.

"Not in our school," Crystal said.

"We could use a real hero now," Cami said.

"Real heroes come from real people. People who usually never plan to become heroes," Dr. Cohen said. Then he looked directly at Cami and Crystal. "You've already rescued this little fellow. He could have died in that dumpster. Or, he could have been crushed when the dumpster was emptied. Looks to me like we have some real heroes, right here."

"Carrie," Mrs. Cohen said, "your mother is on the phone. She's been looking all over for you. She sounded pretty upset. She wants you home right away."

"I'd better get home too," Cami said looking worried, "before I'm late. My mom is probably looking for me too."

"Me, too," Crystal said.

"Meet me back here tomorrow, around noon," David said. "Papa and I will bring the rat to the vet."

I put my right fist out. Crystal put her fist on next, then Cami and David. Then we added our left fists forming an eight-fist-bump power-tower. I looked at my friends and nodded. Then our four voices rang out loud, clear, and strong, "Friends forever, stick together!"

CHAPTER 18
Triple trouble

"We're back," I called out as cheerfully as I could after I opened the front door.

"Do you have *any* idea how worried I've been?" Mom stepped out of the kitchen and put her hands on her hips. Her lips were pursed for a second and she looked right into my eyes. Then Mom's eyes softened. "I called and called. No one answered. I had to leave my job interview early. I called each of your friends trying to track you down. None of their parents had seen you. What were you doing?"

"Carrie's friend found a rat," Kevin said smiling.

"What? You took Kevin to see some rat?" Mom asked, her voice transforming instantly into 'Mean Mom.'

My ears started burning.

"I *had* to go," I said.

"He was white with blue and red spots," Kevin said. "He was sick. I had crackers and grapes."

"You took Kevin to see a sick rat?" Mom asked. "Don't you think you should have checked that out with me first? You didn't even leave a note."

"You don't care. You never care," I screamed. I bolted up the stairs.

"Don't *ever* do that again!" Mom yelled after me.

I threw myself on my bed. I kicked my bed. I kicked the wall. I kicked everything I could reach.

At dinner, I didn't say a word. I cleaned the dishes in silence while Mom put Kevin to bed.

Mom came downstairs.

"I'm going to bed," I said, not looking at her. Then I stomped up the stairs.

That night, I thrashed in my bed. Questions kept swirling in my mind. *Why is Mom always so mad at me? What would Principal Pratt do to Ms. Kramer? What was wrong with the little rat? Why didn't Dad come back? Didn't he care about us?* I had no answers, just more questions and lots of 'should haves'. *I should have stopped their fights. I should have stayed awake. I should have stopped Dad from leaving.* Knots grew in my belly and turned into pinpricks. I winced as my stomach started to ache. I rolled over and tried lying on my back, on my left side, then my right side. Nothing helped. I kicked my blankets off. I kicked my bed until I was too tired to kick anymore.

When I finally fell asleep, I had my worst nightmare ever. I dreamt I was watching Chad and Connor snicker while Mr. Fricter chuckled and laughed, a deep belly laugh that ended with a growl. I felt my stomach start to ache. In my dream, Mr. Fricter was sitting at the teacher's desk in our classroom scribbling in his red notebook. Then, Mr. Fricter suddenly stood up. He looked like he had grown six inches taller. His hands and fingers had grown longer too. He walked over to my desk and towered over me glaring down into my eyes. I wanted to look away, to run away, but I couldn't turn my head. I couldn't move. Mr. Fricter pointed his index finger at me and bellowed three words, "It's your fault."

Each word came out louder than the one before. I felt my ears burning and my stomach ached. Mr. Fricter's fingers stretched towards my face until I could see the dirt under his nails and in the creases of his skin. My heart started pounding, harder and harder, and then suddenly I was running out of the classroom, covering my ears, running and running as fast as I could go.

I felt myself panting, almost out of breath. I was racing in my dream now, away from school, past my house, down the street.

The houses on either side were a blur. Then, all of a sudden, I saw myself run under the *Listen and Learn* banner at Kevin's preschool. I burst into Kevin's classroom and suddenly froze. I could see myself standing perfectly still. I didn't dare move or even breathe.

In my dream, I saw the little faces of Kevin and his classmates singing a song, only the song had no music. And the little boys and girls had no smiles. And, on each of their faces, I could see my own mask, tight lips, tight cheeks, tight eyes.

"Don't talk. Don't ask," the children sang out as if they were reciting a children's rhyme. "In this school, we all wear a mask."

I felt my eyes widen and my mouth opening. I wanted to tell the little boys and girls to sing and dance and play, but nothing came out of my mouth. I had no air in my lungs, no way to speak out.

The children kept on chanting, "We *don't* laugh, we *don't* cry. It's not important to ever know *why*." The children's teacher turned toward me. She looked strangely like Mr. Fricter only her hair was a little longer, stiff and brittle like a sharp wire brush. Her eyes looked like small dark beads. Her face had large blotches. And her nose looked sharper, almost pointed.

"Well done, children. Well done," the teacher said through pursed lips. "Now, line up, tallest to shortest."

I felt myself take a deep breath. My legs started moving in my dream, strong, steady and fast, the way I ran when I played soccer. I ran over to Kevin and hugged him tight.

"Let's go, Kevin," I said in my dream. Kevin looked up at me with his big eyes and chunky cheeks. He put his hand in mine and smiled.

"Let's go," I said again. The teacher glared at me and her pursed lips opened wide exposing dark stained teeth. I stared back. I knew I had to get Kevin out. And somehow, I knew I couldn't be stopped. Not by all the Fricters in the whole world.

I held Kevin's hand. We walked out of the classroom, our heads held high, looking straight ahead. We walked out of the school and into the sunshine. I felt warm and proud inside. Then I woke up. The sun was coming through my window. It was just a dream.

When I walked downstairs, I heard Mom talking on the telephone. I froze and listened. Mom sounded angry. I ran back up to my bedroom and slammed the door. I threw myself on my bed.

I thought I had lost my mother another job. Mom hated me. She would never let me see Cami and Crystal again.

I felt myself start to cry into my pillow. But I didn't care. I would lie there forever. That seemed better than facing another rotten day. Somehow, I drifted off to sleep.

"Carrie, wake up!" Mom said. "It's almost noon. Are you sick?"

"I'm fine," I said. But Mom came in the room and felt my forehead anyway.

"I've got to go to the grocery. I'm taking Kevin," Mom said softly.

"Whatever," I said and pulled myself out of bed. "I'm going outside."

"Leave a note where you go," Mom said and left the room.

I got some cereal for breakfast. I looked out the window and saw David and his grandfather playing catch again. I quickly ate and put on my sneakers and a coat. I scribbled a quick note and ran outside.

"Here's a glove," Dr. Cohen said, tossing his baseball glove to me. He smiled. "I could use some help."

"What happened with the little rat?" I asked.

"He'll be okay. He's in good hands," Dr. Cohen said. "The Animal Hospital vet agreed with me. The bruises were faded but they looked like fingerprints. She took some photos and she's putting your little rat on a special diet to get him drinking and eating again. He'll be fine."

"What about Principal Pratt? Is she going to fire Ms. Kramer?" I asked.

"She said she would find out what happened."

"Did she blame Cami and Crystal or David?"

"No. She said she was glad the rat was okay. But the school board received several complaints about Ms. Kramer. The school board is going to decide what to do next."

"Cami and Crystal called. They're coming over soon," David said. "You can be my catcher until they come."

"No way," I said. "But I'll take you on with a soccer ball any time."

"Great. You two play. My hand hurts and I could use the rest," Dr. Cohen said sounding relieved.

I felt more like myself kicking the soccer ball. I felt even better when Crystal and Cami arrived. We divided up into teams. Crystal and I scored 18 goals to Cami and David's ten. That felt good.

David's grandmother invited all of us to have some lunch. I was surprised how hungry I was and gobbled up two large sandwiches and a bowl of vegetable soup. After lunch, we went outside and sat down at the picnic table in David's backyard.

"I heard Papa talking to Principal Pratt about what's been going on," David said. "They didn't know I was listening. Turns out Papa and Principal Pratt know each other from way back. She was my father's fourth grade teacher."

"She must be really old," Crystal said.

"Pratt was talking about how much things have changed. How the new school board president got rid of music and art, advanced science classes, enrichment programs to save money. How they had to *teach for the tests* each year. The fifth-grade state exam is a big one. This year, every school has to do well on state exams or lose money. And Bartonsville Elementary hasn't been doing well the last two years."

"I miss music class," Cami said frowning.

"I heard Pratt say something about a school board meeting next Wednesday," David said. "The school board president was upset about some letters and phone calls. Some parents complained Ms. Kramer was wasting time, not helping students learn enough math, reading, social studies, science. Some parents complained their children were scared, that Ms. Kramer was talking about things fifth graders shouldn't hear about."

"Like what?" I asked.

"Like frogs dying. Sounded like Ms. Kramer is in big trouble."

"That stinks," Crystal said.

"Principal Pratt said that two boys' parents have been writing letters saying their sons were being unfairly picked on, kept after school for no good reason, forced to do too much work on stuff that wasn't going to be on the state exams. Bet we know who those boys are! Mr. Fricter filed a complaint about how his detention of three girls was dismissed. And then, there was the missing rat. One girl's mother called, said she and other parents were worried about diseases that could be spread by rats in the school. They're afraid of all kinds of stuff, rats biting, rat diseases, plagues ... crazy stuff like that."

"Messed up," Crystal said.

"Papa asked what would happen to Ms. Kramer. Pratt thinks the school board president wants to use Ms. Kramer as a lesson to other teachers. *Run your class the way the school board president wants or leave.* The school board president won't even let Ms. Kramer come to the meeting Wednesday."

"Doesn't she have a union, or something, to help her?" Cami asked.

"She's just a substitute teacher. She can be fired any time the school board wants."

"Totally messed up," Crystal said.

I thought about that for a moment and looked at my friends.

"Remember when Ms. Kramer asked us why heroes wear masks?" My friends nodded. "This is why."

"What are you talking about?" Crystal asked.

"Don't you see?" I said. "Ms. Kramer made our class better. And she got in trouble. She didn't hide what she did. Sometimes, heroes hide who they really are, so they can keep doing good things. Heroes wear masks because if you try to make things better, if you try to make changes, some people will go after you. Some people don't want things to change."

"Like Mr. Fricter," Cami said. "I've never seen him so happy as the last few days with Ms. Kramer gone."

"My grandfather used to say, 'if you stick your head up, you'll be shot at'," Crystal said nodding. "It's something he learned in the Army."

"So, what do we do?" Cami asked.

"We *have* to help Ms. Kramer," I said.

"How?" Crystal asked.

"We need a lawyer," Cami said.

My shoulders sagged. I looked down at the dirt and grass.

"What?" Cami asked.

"Nothing," I said.

"What?" Cami asked again.

I felt a tear coming and turned my head away. I felt another tear coming. I turned away from my friends and kicked the ground hard enough to send grass flying.

"Tell us," Cami said. "You're always talking about how people don't say what's real anymore. How people are afraid to tell the truth." She sat close to me.

"And we're not just any people," Crystal said, coming over to sit next to me on the other side.

I shook my head. I couldn't let down my mask, even just a little. *Not now. Not ever.*

"Tell us," Cami said again, putting her arm around my shoulders. "It will be okay. You can tell us."

I kept looking down and kicked the grass harder.

"We can help," Cami said softly.

"You can't help," I said. My voice became louder and angrier. "It's not okay. It's not going to be okay."

Cami gently hugged me from my right side and Crystal held me close on my left. I wanted to break free and run away but I couldn't move. I felt my mask slipping. I gulped some air. Then the tears came. First, a few drops, then a rainstorm. I gave up fighting to hold it all inside.

"My mom and dad used to fight. Lots of fights. I'd stay up to make sure they were okay. But one night I fell asleep. I didn't stop them. My Dad left. I should have stopped him. If I had, he'd be alive."

I kicked the grass again.

"And Mom got laid off. She hates me. I messed up her chance to get a new job last week. I lost my dad. All I do is mess up."

I kicked the grass again, even harder this time. This time I tore a hole in the ground kicking a clump of dirt high up into the air.

"Now, they're going to fire Ms. Kramer. Everything's a mess. I hate this stink-hole town!"

I kept kicking the grass. I couldn't stop.

No one said anything. I shuddered inside. Cami and Crystal just kept on hugging me. After a while, my tears ran out. I stopped kicking.

"Maybe one person can't change things but a whole team has a chance," David said.

"Dork!" I yelled, looking at the holes I had dug with my kicks. Then I glared at David. "You don't know zip. Your parents are okay. You're going to leave this town. You're not stuck like us!"

"Maybe he has a point," Crystal said softly.

"We're a team," Cami said.

"*The Three Cs* plus David," Crystal said with a quick shy smile.

"We'll figure out a plan to bring back Ms. Kramer," Cami said. "We will."

"Huddle time," Crystal said. I still looked down at the dirt, but I could feel the warmth of my friends' arms around me. Part of me wanted to hide. Part of me wanted to run away. Part of me wanted to believe my friends.

"Fists out," Cami said standing up.

I felt myself rise up and added two fists to my friends' six.

"Friends forever," Crystal said.

"Stick together!" Cami and David said.

I lifted my head up and saw my friends around me. They hadn't given up. Somehow, I felt stronger again. And suddenly, I had a plan. I started walking back to my house.

"Where are you going?" Cami asked.

"This team needs a coach. I've got a call to make," I said.

CHAPTER 19

S O S

Mom and Kevin were working on a puzzle when I walked into the kitchen.

"Dinner's at 6:00," Mom said.

"Okay," I said and went upstairs. I picked up the phone in Mom's bedroom and called Uncle Phil. I would get him to help Ms. Kramer. The receptionist connected me to his office. The phone rang and rang and rang. The voice mail came on. I hung up and called again. I got the voice mail again. I called another time.

"Hello," my uncle finally said. He sounded tired. But, then, he often sounded that way.

"It's me, Carrie."

"What's going on? Are you okay? Are Kevin and your Mom okay?"

"We're okay. But I need your help." I told him about how Ms. Kramer was teaching us about heroes and standing up for others, some of the same things Dad used to talk about at home. Then, I told him about the missing little rat, how Ms. Kramer was put 'on leave,' how my friends found the missing rat, the bruises on the rat, how Mr. Fricter had been taking notes, how he and some parents complained to the school board president, the school board meeting on Wednesday, and how horrible Mr. Fricter was leading the class.

"Principal Pratt is going to fire Ms. Kramer," I said.

"Well, the school will have to show some serious problems with her teaching or prove there was insubordination, that Ms. Kramer was defying school policies," my uncle said. His voice was way too calm. He didn't get it.

"The school board president is trying to get rid of Ms. Kramer. She's a great teacher. Shouldn't she have a lawyer? Can't you help her?"

"Carrie, I've got to be in court Monday, Tuesday, and Wednesday. Even if I didn't, I'm not licensed to serve as an attorney in your state."

"Please ..."

"I'm sorry Carrie. I'm not licensed. I'm not the right ..."

"You're no help!"

"Carrie, I can't be her lawyer."

I didn't say anything.

"Let me talk to your Mom."

"She's busy with Kevin." I slammed the phone down hard.

A minute later, the phone rang. I ran into my room and slammed the door. I heard Mom talking downstairs. The sound of her voice came up through the heating vents, something my parents never figured out. It was a good way for me to listen in on their conversations. Only, today, I didn't want to hear what Mom said.

Mom's voice stopped. I heard footsteps, tired, slow footsteps coming up the stairs. There was a knock on my door.

"Go away!" I said.

"Carrie ..."

"Just go away!"

Mom opened the door.

"Why'd you hang up on your uncle?"

"What do you care? We could have moved near him, like Dad wanted. Now, we're stuck here!"

"Carrie, come down for dinner."

"I'm not hungry!" I yelled into my pillow.

"What did you say?"

I lifted my head and yelled louder now.

"I hate this stinkin' place!"

"Carrie ..."

"GET OUT!" I buried my head in my pillow. "Go away. Leave me alone. Leave me a-l-o-n-e!" A few minutes later, I heard the door close.

On Sunday morning, I looked in the mirror. Tight lips, tight cheeks, tight eyes. Mask in place. I didn't say a word to Mom or Kevin the whole day.

My uncle called. I shook my head when Mom told me who was calling.

"Pick up the phone," Mom said.

I went into Mom's bedroom and picked up the phone.

"What?" I asked in a not-so-nice tone that I hoped would drive my uncle far away.

"I can't be your teacher's lawyer. But I have been thinking about this. And I feel very bad about not being able to get to the school board meeting."

"Whatever."

"I don't really know what's going on. But I know you're glad you had Ms. Kramer and I wouldn't be surprised if other students feel the same way."

"So what?"

"So, I remember what your dad used to say to me. A good lawyer looks for what's missing, as much as what is known. A good lawyer listens for *what's not said, what's not said that needs to be said.* That's one way lawyers can help. And *what's missing* often is people, or in this case, students, speaking up. Kids getting their message to the right people in the right way, a way that can speak to what's really going on."

"Who cares what kids think? No one!"

"It's a lot harder to fire a popular teacher than an unpopular one. School boards are elected. And even if children don't vote, each child in your class has parents who do vote."

"So what?"

"So, if Principal Pratt is making the decision then she's like a judge or a jury in a court case."

"Why should Pratt care what we think? She's just working for the school board." Then, I screamed into the phone. "She's going to fire Ms. Kramer!"

My uncle was silent for a few seconds.

"Well, we don't really know what she wants to do, do we? Maybe you and your friends can give her some reasons not to fire Ms. Kramer."

I pictured Principal Pratt's face. Tight lips, tight eyes, tight cheeks, little lines running from the corners of her eyes. It was another mask. Or, maybe that was her real face. I shuddered inside and wondered. Maybe if you wear your mask too long, it becomes your real face. I shuddered again. It could happen to me too.

My uncle went on.

"From what I heard, it sounds like some parents have been complaining about how Ms. Kramer was teaching, saying she wasn't teaching the subjects she was required to teach, saying she taught things that were not in the new curriculum, saying she endangered children in the class, like with the rat."

"The little rat was *never* a danger! And we did *all* the subjects with Ms. Kramer. Just as much as before. She just made it fun."

"So, to help Ms. Kramer," my uncle continued, "a lawyer would want to show the opposite of the complaints, how Ms. Kramer was teaching the subjects she needed to teach, how she was keeping the class safe. People may have been scared of little rats because they really didn't know much about little rats. People may have been scared about a new teacher because they didn't really know what she was teaching."

"So what?"

"So, a good lawyer wants the judge to know the facts that help her client. A good lawyer wants to know how the judge thinks and help the judge see her clients' side of the story. Principal Pratt didn't stop Ms. Kramer from bringing the rats to school, right?

"I guess so."

"So, she's probably not afraid of rats. She also was a teacher once herself. So, she knows what it's like to help children learn. Principal Pratt's job is to make sure she has good teachers teaching every class and students are learning. And who knows better about what good work Ms. Kramer was doing and how much students were really learning than the students?"

All of this sounded like too much. I thought of Principal Pratt standing in the back of the classroom, watching Mr. Fricter lead the class. You couldn't tell what she was thinking. She didn't show any sign of really caring.

"If Principal Pratt cared at all, she would never have left us with Mr. Fricter."

"Carrie ..."

"I've got to go." I hung up before he could say anything else. I spent the rest of the day in my room, leaving only for lunch and dinner. And, even then, I hardly said a word.

In school on Monday, Aliesha asked Mr. Fricter if he wanted their papers on how heroes got past fears and she asked him if she could still get extra points for her report about why heroes wear masks.

"Keep your papers. And there will be no extra points," Mr. Fricter said. "I'll tell you why people wear masks. Real simple. Real life is different than comic book stories. In real life, people wear masks because they're afraid of anyone finding out who they really are. They're scared to show their faces. Or else, they know they did something wrong, something bad. They're hiding. Case closed. Now, open your social studies books to page 187." He smiled his crooked half-smile and pointed his index finger at Aliesha. "You can be the first to read out loud." I noticed that his fingernail was longer and dirtier than ever.

The rest of Monday was just as bad. Mr. Fricter yelled at Crystal for being out of her seat when she just went to sharpen her pencil. He pointed his finger at her and I was sure Crystal was going to get detention or worse. But, before he could say anything, the door opened. Principal Pratt walked in and stood in the back of the room.

Mr. Fricter quickly put on his kind, caring face and told the class to "please do their math work" and how he'd be available to help them with any questions. Principal Pratt then went up to Mr. Fricter and quietly asked if she could see the students' heroes' papers from the previous weekend.

"Uhh, I gave them another week to work on them," Mr. Fricter said, his eyes shifting left and right. Principal Pratt just looked at him then left the room.

Later that morning, Mr. Fricter announced that he was starting a new class routine. Each week, he'd pick a 'Student of the Week,' to get special honors and help him, a student who had done something special for the class. "For this week," he said smiling and nodding at Chad, "I've selected Chad, a student who has shown exemplary progress."

Chad smiled back at Mr. Fricter with a sweet look on his face.

Crystal groaned.

"Problem today, young lady?" Mr. Fricter asked.

Crystal shook her head.

"Okay, Chad will pass out worksheets. We've got a lot of math and social studies to cover today, and a double vocabulary lesson. I want to show the school board how *much* we can get done by Wednesday. So, children, listen and learn. Listen *and* learn."

A few minutes later, Principal Pratt returned to the class.

"The school board president has asked for two students to speak at a special school board meeting this Wednesday afternoon," she said. "Parents are invited as well. The meeting will take place right after school in our gym. The school board president is running the meeting. She wants to hear what it's been like in this class from students as well as from teachers and parents."

Connor's arm shot up immediately.

"I'd be very honored to represent the class, Principal Pratt."

Mr. Fricter nodded and smiled.

"I would too," I said quickly, surprising myself.

No one else volunteered.

"Very good," Principal Pratt said and left the room.

All the rest of that day and on the bus ride home, I thought about what I'd say. I thought of all the arguments I'd make.

"Carrie," Mom said from the kitchen. Her voice sounded cheerful, even happy. "Good news! I've got a new job. It's a good job, better than my last one, much better, *much much better!*"

"That's great," I said. I put my backpack down and sat at the kitchen table. Mom was cutting vegetables for dinner and cooking homemade macaroni and cheese. "I have news too. Principal Pratt asked for volunteers to speak at a special school board meeting Wednesday, right after school. It's about all the complaints about Ms. Kramer. I was picked to go. Parents can come too."

"I got an e mail about the meeting," Mom said. "But, Carrie, I can't go this Wednesday. They said they need me to start this Wednesday at my new job. That's a big day for my new company. They're starting a new project and I'm supposed to help them that afternoon when the TV reporters come. It should be on the news Wednesday night. I promised them I'd be there and I'd be able to stay late. It's a big reason they hired me. I really need you to get Kevin after school that day. Just this one more time. Next week, I'll be able to pay for extra hours at his school and then I can get him myself. Can't another student speak to the school board?"

"The other boy who's going hates Ms. Kramer."

"I'm sorry honey."

"I *have* to go, Mom."

"Carrie, I have to get this job. We need the money I will make from this job. Sometimes we can't do what we want to do."

"You don't understand."

"Carrie, I can't, I ..."

"You don't care! You never care!" I grabbed my backpack and stomped up the stairs. I slammed the door to my bedroom and threw myself on my bed. A few minutes later, Mom knocked on the door but I wouldn't answer. A little while later, I heard Mom leave to pick up Kevin from his school.

I looked over at my dresser. I noticed a photo of Cami and me from second grade. We both looked so happy, playing on a beach, tossing a ball to each other. I remembered that our families had taken a vacation together that year.

I wished things could have just stayed like they were. Then, I remembered Ms. Kramer talking about how things changed for everybody and how most people struggled sooner or later. Ms. Kramer told the class that even geniuses got frustrated. When Einstein couldn't figure something out, he would play or listen to classical music, Bach or something.

I put on my favorite song. I listened to the singers' voices grow stronger and stronger. I could feel their determination. They wouldn't give up and neither would I. I took a breath, then another, gradually slowing my breaths down as I felt my belly rise with each breath. I remembered how the class had practiced SOS for Stress[1] for times when heroes were in trouble. It was a way to cool down and slow down enough to figure out what to do next, a way to become more like our favorite heroes when they faced trouble. "S" was a reminder to slow down their breathing, counting slowly "1, 2, 3" as they breathed in and "3, 2, 1" as they let the air back out.[2] "O" meant opening their eyes to who and what could help them. And the last "S" reminded heroes to seek help and help others.

I felt the air going in and out of my body, slower now, steady and strong. I imagined the air flowing like liquid energy down from my mouth into my lungs, into my chest, down into my legs, down to my ankles and toes and then back up my body and out again. Then, I took another breath and imagined the liquid energy flowing this time from my mouth into my shoulders, down my arms, through my hands to my fingertips and then back up my hands, arms, shoulders and out again as I exhaled. I took ten long slow breaths and with each breath, I felt stronger and stronger.

SOS

I was stretching out with my feelings. Alex would like that. Then, I remembered some of the other things the class had learned. How heroes had to struggle to get past their fears so they could help other people. How heroes often felt they were stuck, trapped. And I remembered my classes' *Secrets of Heroes* to get unstuck, to keep moving in 'tough times.'

We also talked about fear. How fears can make you do things without thinking like run away, fight, or freeze and how fears can get worse, the more stuck you feel.

Aliesha said fear was like poison.

"You need an antidote," Cami said.

"You need to do something," I said, "to get away or fight."

"But how do you muster the courage to do something when you're scared?" Ms. Kramer asked.

"If you believe it needs to be done, then you do it," I said. "Whatever it takes."

The class had come up with ways to get past fear. Then, Ms. Kramer talked about using fear itself as energy, to welcome fear rather than fighting it.

I remembered how heroes kept going when 'the going got tough,' when 'hard times' dragged on and on, when other people gave up, when hope flickered like a dying candle. And heroes didn't do it by themselves. They helped each other, like Cami, Crystal, David and me.

I remembered how Cami and I had gotten all the kids in our third-grade class to sign a letter asking for a longer morning recess after recess time had been cut back. Then, Cami and I had marched up to the principal's office and handed the letter to him. We had a different principal back then, Principal Feinman. Principal Feinman read the letter carefully. He laughed, but it was a nice laugh, and his eyes twinkled.

"I'll take this petition under advisement," he said, whatever that meant. Still, I felt good for trying.

And a funny thing happened. Principal Feinman stopped by to check on Cami and me the next day and almost every week after that. He would also smile at us as we entered the school building.

"Ready for another great day at school, Carrie, Cami?" he'd ask with a grin. And the funny thing was, my whole day at school seemed better. Even recess seemed better. Cami and I ran outside faster and we had more fun, even with the shorter time.

Later that school year, Cami and I handed Principal Feinman another letter. Just two students, Cami and me, signed this one. Cami always brought her lunch to school. So, I had asked Cami why she never ate the food from the cafeteria.

"That's because they never serve anything for vegetarians. I don't eat meat and that's all they give us," Cami said.

I had never thought about it. Cami and her whole family never ate meat. That's when I came up with the idea of another letter.

My father was always saying things like, 'Let the record show,' to make his point. Usually his point was that he was right and that Kevin, Mom and I should listen to him more. Like how he had told us to pack for rain on a trip. No one listened and we all got soaked. "Let the record show," my father said to remind us as we stood there dripping wet.

My father had also taught me that it was always a good idea to get things in writing. That way, people were more likely to pay attention and give your ideas some serious thought. And if people didn't do what they said they'd do, you'd have proof to back you up.

"No matter what happens," I told Cami as we walked to Principal Feinman's office, "let the record show, we tried to make school lunches fair."

"Come on in," Principal Feinman said, waving his arm and smiling. "What do you have for me today. Another petition?"

I handed the letter to Principal Feinman. He read it over carefully, then scratched the side of his head.

"Thank you," he said. "Thank you for bringing this to my attention." And he smiled at Cami and me. "Stop by anytime."

We left the office.

"He probably won't do anything," I said.

"I know," Cami said. "He'll say he doesn't control the cafeteria. Some department of the school administration runs it. They have their own rules. Blah. Blah. Blah. Whatever!" But three weeks later, a surprising thing happened. On the menu board at the bottom, under the fried chicken and green beans listed for lunch that day, a note said, "Attention students. Starting Monday, a vegetarian meal will be provided every day."

I smiled as I remembered this little victory. But then I remembered how things changed after Principal Feinman left. In the fourth grade, I asked my teacher why the school stopped teaching art and music. I liked art and I loved music. Ms. Rey, my teacher, said it was because they needed to use the time for more work on Math and English.

"Why do we need more time for Math and English?" I asked Ms. Rey in front of the entire class. No one else said anything. No one dared. Ms. Rey had a look that scared most of the students. Cami and I called it 'Ms. Rey's X-Ray.' No one looked at Ms. Rey when she put on her X-Ray eyes and no one asked her questions, no one that is except me.

"The school board wants students in this school to do better on the Math and English tests," Ms. Rey said. "The president of the school board said our scores were 'an embarrassment to the whole town.' People won't want to live here with students getting test scores like these. The school board president said it was up to the schools to show the world this was a good place to live. And that means all of you doing better on Math and English tests."

"I miss Music and Art. Music and Art are important, too, you know," I said. The other kids looked at me like I was nuts. I was criticizing a school decision. I was talking back to a teacher. I was talking back to Ms. Rey, of all the teachers, the one you never talked back to!

Ms. Rey put on her X-Ray eyes and focused them on me. "Not as important as doing better on the Math and English tests," she said slowly and pursed her lips, letting her eyes burn into me for what seemed like forever. Then she made a note in her red folder, the folder where she put all the students' grades. The same folder where she wrote a note each time I got a detention for not being able to sit still in her class and talking even when Ms. Rey said to work quietly.

I heard the door open downstairs. Mom was back with Kevin. I heard Mom go into the kitchen and get Kevin a snack.

"Game's not over," I said to myself. I would not be stopped. I called Cami. Cami talked to her mother. Then, I called Crystal and David. In no time, I had a plan. I was ready to go.

Notes

1 Adapted from Ford, J. and Russo, E. (2006). TARGET; A Trauma-Focused, Present-Centered, Emotional Self-Regulation Approach to Integrated Treatment for Post-Traumatic Stress and Addiction: Trauma Adaptive Recovery Group Education and Therapy (TARGET). *American Journal of Psychotherapy* and Kagan R. *(2017). Real Life Heroes Toolkit for Treating Traumatic Stress in Children and Families, 2nd Edition,* New York: Routledge.
2 Adapted from Briere, J. (2011). Mindfulness and Complex Trauma therapy. NCTSN Webcast, January, 2011. {www.nctsn.org}

CHAPTER 20

Two hundred problems

I waited for Mom to put away Kevin's backpack and clean out his lunch box. I heard her give Kevin a puzzle to work on and sit down to check the mail. Then, I joined her, sitting quietly.

"I'm sorry I yelled," I said softly.

Mom nodded.

"And for what I said."

Mom sighed.

"I have a plan for Wednesday." I told Mom that Cami's mother said she could pick up Kevin and watch him until Mom or I could get him. "Kevin knows Cami's mom. He likes her."

"I don't like asking another parent for help."

"Please ..."

Mom sighed again and shook her head.

"Okay, this time. But next time ask me before you call another parent."

I nodded.

"Can I use your laptop? I need to look up some phone numbers. I need to talk to some kids in my class."

"About what?"

"Homework. I also need the computer to finish a class project."

Mom nodded and I dashed back upstairs.

Tuesday seemed to fly by in a flash. I often felt like I was being watched, but when I looked up from my desk, Mr. Fricter seemed busy reading or lecturing another student. Principal Pratt kept going in and out of the classroom so often that I sometimes was surprised to find her in the back of the classroom without my even knowing she had returned.

On Wednesday morning, Mom rushed around at hyper speed getting Kevin and herself ready for work.

"I'm running late. First day, and I'm running late," Mom kept saying, a nervous look on her face. She grabbed Kevin with one hand. She picked up his backpack, his lunch box, and her shoulder bag with the other. "Carrie, lock the door when you leave. Bye, Hon. I'll be thinking of you today. Oh, no, I'm late. Got to go ..."

I heard the door close.

"Whatever," I said half out loud. I took a deep breath and grabbed my backpack. It was 'Go time'. I left the house.

Mr. Fricter seemed especially happy that day. He wore a brightly colored tie and had his greasy hair slicked back.

"We have a special guest this morning," he said. "I'm delighted to have the President of the Bartonsville School Board, Ms. Thurman, join us. She can only stay a few minutes. So, let's begin by handing in your vocabulary papers and then we'll show her what you've learned. I've told Ms. Thurman that you've been mastering a double lesson this week. I'm so very proud of each and every one of you." Mr. Fricter smiled his crooked smile at Ms. Thurman who stood at the back of the room. She nodded back at him.

"Chad, please pick up the papers," Mr. Fricter said in a gentle voice.

Chad walked from desk to desk but only ten students handed in their homework out of the class of 24.

"It's vocabulary quiz time," Mr. Fricter said. He read the vocabulary words from his list and asked the students to spell each word and write what the word meant. Ms. Thurman walked around the room as the students worked at their desks. I could see her smile turn into a frown as she read over the students' work. At the same time, Mr. Fricter seemed to be struggling to keep up his crooked half-smile. His smile disappeared 20 minutes later, after Ms. Thurman left the room. Mr. Fricter pursed his lips and daggers appeared to fly from his eyes.

Mr. Fricter waved the ten papers he received from the class like a paper sword slashing in the air. "Fourteen missing papers. Ten papers with errors. You're *all* flunking this quiz. I should keep you all after school today ..."

Mr. Fricter stopped himself. He rubbed his hands together and his crooked half-smile returned.

"But that can wait. I've got other business this afternoon."

Then he sat down clasping one hand over the other and rubbing them back and forth. First, he rubbed the backs of his hands, then he rubbed the palms of his hands. And, all the while, his crooked half-smile grew larger and larger.

"Math homework for the rest of the day," Mr. Fricter said.

Then, he returned to his fake sweet voice.

"Chad, won't you please pass out today's math problems? I believe there are about 200. That should keep everyone busy. And, to show how kind I am, anyone who needs extra help, will stay after school with Mr. Jones next door until I get back from the school board meeting. Then, I'll be 'oh so *very* glad' to supervise you myself, for *as long as it takes*."

Mr. Fricter scanned the room making sure to glare at every student, except two, Chad and Connor, who gazed up at Mr. Fricter with their sweet faces. When Mr. Fricter got to me, he stopped, glared into my eyes, and pointed his finger right at me.

"Any questions?" he asked in his fake sweet voice. "I'm certainly looking forward to helping all of you for the rest of the school year. All right, get to work!"

I wondered why people said monsters weren't real. And then, once again, I felt like someone was watching me.

Principal Pratt walked in the room. I quickly looked down at the math worksheet. I wondered if the principal had been watching through the window in the door. My shoulders sagged when I saw how hard the math problems were but I got right to work. I wasn't going to miss the school board meeting. I even worked through recess period. My friends did as well. By the time the bell rang, I had completed all 200 problems. I dropped them on Mr. Fricter's desk.

Mr. Fricter scowled at me.

"I know how to deal with kids like you. I used to work in a lock-up for kids who assaulted adults." Then, he glared at me. "Don't get any ideas in my class. I'll be watching."

I stared right back at him through my mask. I really wanted to kick him but I knew that's just what he wanted. That would prove he was right about me. So, I just turned and left the room.

CHAPTER 21
All alone

I walked to the school gym and opened the door. It didn't seem like the same gym I had known for the last six years. Rows of chairs filled the gym. A large table with 12 chairs had been set up at the front of the left side of the stage and a smaller table with two chairs was set up on the right side. Each table had one microphone. Men and women I had never seen before were standing around talking. The men standing near the large table wore suits and ties. The women wore dresses or pantsuits. They all wore dark colored clothes. None of them looked happy to be there.

Up on the stage, Connor was shaking the hand of Ms. Thurman, the school board president. She smiled at Connor. A large man stood behind Connor with his hand on Connor's shoulder. The man had short hair, broad shoulders and a large belly that bulged out of his dark gray suit. He looked a lot like Connor. The man turned his head and looked at the people coming into the gym with hard eyes and pursed lips that seemed to say, 'Don't mess with me or my son.' Suddenly, I felt the man's eyes lock onto mine. Then I saw Connor and Ms. Thurman turn and glare in my direction.

My stomach started to ache like it had been pierced by a thousand pinpricks. I suddenly felt all alone. No father. No mother around. I didn't know where to go. For a moment, my legs locked up stiff, unable to move. I felt a teardrop grow in my right eye. *What was I doing here? How could I go up on that stage alone?*

I looked back at the gym door. I could run out. Why did I have to be the one? My right leg started stomping the floor, again and again, harder and harder. I looked down. I took a deep breath. I knew what my leg was telling me. I had to get up on that stage to save the best teacher I ever had. I had to get up on that stage to save my class from the horrible teacher's aide who would take over when she was gone. I had to get up on that stage because I had failed so badly before.

I shook my head hard to the left. The teardrop flew out into the air. I checked my face: tight lips, tight cheeks, tight eyes. Then, I lifted my head. It was go-time.

"We'll be in the front row," a cheery voice called out from behind me. I turned and saw Cami smiling at me. David and Crystal were with her. And, behind them, Cami's father, Crystal's mother, and David's grandparents.

"Remember, 'Friends forever ...'," Cami said, giving me a quick hug.

I took a super-deep breath and stepped onto the stage. Principal Pratt directed me to a row of chairs on the far-right side of the stage behind the smaller table. Connor sat on one of the other chairs with his father next to him. Connor looked past me and smiled at a large heavyset woman sitting in the front row on the far side of the gym. She wore large silver earrings, a sparkling necklace, and a black dress. The woman smiled and nodded at Connor. I felt my stomach start to ache.

I sat down leaving an empty chair between Connor and me. Then, I saw my friends looking up at me from the front row on the side of the gym closest to me. Crystal smiled and held up two fists, one on top of the other, a two-fisted power bump salute. Crystal's mother sat next to her left along with David and his grandparents. Cami sat next to her father, smiling up at me with her two fists raised up, one on top of the other, just like Crystal.

A microphone squealed as Ms. Thurman began talking through the gym speakers.

"This is a special meeting to address serious concerns that have come to my attention about implementation of the fifth-grade curriculum at Bartonsville Elementary and concerns raised by parents of students in Classroom 5D." She nodded towards Connor's father and then to a thin woman sitting next to Chad who I figured was Chad's mother. Chad and his mother were sitting up front on the right side of the gym next to the heavy-set woman Connor had been smiling at. I could also see Theresa sitting with her mother in the row behind them.

"As you know," Ms. Thurman said in a stern and commanding voice, "I directed the superintendent to start a new elementary school curriculum two years ago. This curriculum emphasized teaching Literary Arts, Mathematics, Science, and Social Studies. Teachers were directed to prepare their students for state exams and to emphasize discipline in the classroom. 'Zero tolerance' would be enforced for all behavior problems. Each school would compete with other schools to see whose students did best. The most successful schools would be rewarded and failing schools would be penalized." Ms. Thurman smiled and then went on.

"We also did away with those all-too expensive special classes that took away time from these core subjects. As you probably noticed, each school was given a banner to welcome students into our new educational programs, programs in which they would *Listen and Learn to Achieve.*"

Ms. Thurman nodded and smiled as though, she was accepting applause for a great triumph she had achieved, the creation of a model school system and the answer to all the town's problems. She scanned over the silent gym nodding to a half dozen adults in the seats below. Then, she turned and looked right at Principal Pratt.

"This spring," Ms. Thurman said, her voice taking on a hard edge, "I was alerted by three parents and two faculty members about problems at Bartonsville Elementary. We lost a fine fifth-grade teacher who believed in the same high standards that I do. This teacher told me privately before she left that she had been repeatedly criticized by her principal for her strident efforts to teach the new curriculum. She felt so criticized and so unsupported that she left. After that teacher departed, I received letters and calls from parents and a teacher's aide about violations of school policies in this teacher's former classroom, Classroom 5D."

Ms. Thurman's voice took on an angry edge now.

"Problems continued and I directed Principal Pratt to conduct an evaluation of the substitute teacher we had brought in to complete the school year. I asked Principal Pratt to make absolutely certain that core subjects were being taught *exactly* as indicated in the new curriculum."

Ms. Thurman shook her head from side to side, frowning as she went on.

"Despite these directives, I kept hearing complaints about the new teacher."

She looked down at some papers.

"Problems cited by parents and the teacher's aide included taking away time from core subjects and working instead on a special project of questionable value, inappropriately terminating the detention of three disruptive students, and singling out two boys described as model students and giving them unfair detentions. Parents also complained that their children were upset about their new teacher telling them about frogs being killed and little rats being abused in what one student called, and I quote, 'a terrible experiment by mean scientists that scared me and my friends.'" Ms. Thurman shook her sad.

"And then, last week, we had a serious safety risk for students when a potentially diseased rat was reported missing and presumably loose in the classroom. This potentially diseased rat was brought to school by the new teacher with authorization from Principal Pratt."

Ms. Thurman shook her head scornfully again and slowly gazed around the gym as if she wanted to share her scorn personally with each adult in the gym. Then she drilled her eyes into Principal Pratt.

"We will now address these critical issues in three steps: First, a public meeting on what can be done to help the students of Classroom 5D. Second, a closed meeting of the school board to address terminating our contract with the substitute teacher."

Ms. Thurman paused.

"And third, a decision by the school board about whether a change in leadership is necessary at Bartonsville Elementary."

I saw a few parents in the gym suddenly turn their heads and look at Principal Pratt. But Principal Pratt appeared like she always did. Her face was rock hard, steady and serious. She was looking directly ahead of her at the school board members. Her back was straight, her hands were folded on her lap. I knew she had her mask on, just like me.

"For our public meeting, we are going to hear first from our teacher's aide in Classroom 5D, Mr. Fricter, followed by two students, Connor and Carrie, and Principal Pratt. Then, we will invite any members of the public who would like to speak. Ms. Kramer, the Classroom 5D teacher, was put on 'temporary leave' and will not be speaking today. I also regret to say that our school superintendent is ill today and can't be here. So, I will represent her."

Ms. Thurman nodded towards Mr. Fricter and introduced him as the first speaker.

"Mr. Fricter has been a well-regarded teacher's aide for the last four years. I heard many wonderful descriptions of his work by Ms. Craddick, the previous teacher for Classroom 5D. Mr. Fricter, please describe how the required subjects have been taught in Classroom 5D since the loss of Ms. Craddick."

Mr. Fricter winced as he stepped on to the stage. He had put on a sport coat that was tilted to one side. His tie was tilted to the other side making him look rather crooked. He sat down at the small table, nodded to Ms. Thurman and pulled the microphone close to his mouth. His voice boomed out over the speaker system. Mr. Fricter described how he and Ms. Craddick had worked very hard to educate an especially difficult group of students using the new curriculum and how they had established discipline in the classroom.

Mr. Fricter pulled out his red notebook and read from his notes.

"Then, after Ms. Craddick left, the new teacher, Ms. Kramer, changed the class daily schedule. The class lost valuable time for core subjects. Time was spent instead on discussions with students about stories and animals, like frogs and rats. And Ms. Kramer encouraged students to ask questions about our nation's leaders.

"I became very concerned," Mr. Fricter said in a solemn voice, shaking his head slowly and looking across the stage at Ms. Thurman, "about the terrible distress Ms. Kramer created when she forced young children to learn about experiments by scientists who had hurt and killed frogs. Ms. Kramer brought a frog and later rats into the classroom. A rat was lost and the classroom had to be evacuated to maintain safety for the children." Mr. Fricter shook his head again, frowning as he finished talking.

"Thank you," Ms. Thurman said. She smiled and nodded at Mr. Fricter. He left the stage smiling his crooked half-smile. Mr. Fricter took a seat next to Chad's mother.

"Now, we do listen to our students as well as to our parents and our teachers," Ms. Thurman said nodding. She smiled and invited Connor to speak next at the small table. Connor's father joined him, sitting by his side. Connor had his sweet little angel face on. He read from a printed sheet of paper about how some students had been allowed to be disruptive to other students who were trying to learn after Ms. Craddick left.

"Mr. Fricter tried to provide discipline," Connor said, "but our new teacher didn't maintain the rules Ms. Craddick had set for the classroom. That's when things got bad. My friend and I wished we had more time to learn vocabulary and math, like we used to with Ms. Craddick. We wanted to do better on the fifth-grade exams."

Connor nodded towards Chad.

"But Ms. Kramer *made* us put away our textbooks so kids could talk to each other about their favorite heroes and frogs and rats and stuff like that. Fortunately, we still had Mr. Fricter in the class." Connor nodded towards Mr. Fricter as he finished talking. I felt my stomach twinge as I watched Mr. Fricter smile back at Connor.

Ms. Thurman smiled and her eyes seemed to sparkle as she thanked Connor. Connor and his father smiled back at Ms. Thurman, then stood up and went to sit in the front row next to the heavyset woman.

"Next, we have a second student, Carrie Sanderson," Ms. Thurman said, looking at me. Her smile transformed into pursed lips.

I walked to the small table. I had to pull the microphone very hard to get it anywhere near my mouth. A loud noise screeched out of the speakers and I jerked back. I saw several adults staring coldly at me. Ms. Thurman's eyes hardened. Chad and Connor grinned and pretended to clap.

"Go ahead, dear," Ms. Thurman said between pinched lips.

"This is my sixth year at Bartonsville Elementary, my last year."

I felt very small and my voice sounded weak.

"It's been my very worst *and* also my very best year. Before Ms. Kramer came, Classroom 5D felt like a prison. No one talked or asked any questions. No one dared. Everyone looked like they were wearing masks, like they were hiding their true faces."

I could almost feel Ms. Thurman's eyes boring into mine. I heard Chad and Connor snicker. My heart was beating loud.

"And I did it too," I said softly.

"What's that? Speak up," Ms. Thurman thundered through the speaker system. "What did you do?"

I looked up. I remembered how Ms. Kramer taught us to take a slow breath to slow down and grow strong. I saw my friends in the front row. I took a long slow breath.

"Then, Ms. Kramer came."

My voice grew louder now.

"She took Math, Reading, Social Studies, Science and she made them interesting again. She got us to think about things, not just memorize. She got us to do things with this each subject. She got us to think *and* learn. We did all the same subjects but Ms. Kramer made them interesting and fun."

I kept looking at Cami and Crystal.

"Ms. Kramer got us to see how Math, Science, all of our subjects, were important for heroes. We learned how fears keep animals and children from learning. We learned how fear can keep people from talking and asking questions. We've learned so much this Spring!"

"Now, I understand that you have had a number of behavior problems this year," Ms. Thurman said, cutting me off. Her eyes bored deeper into my face. "In fact, I see, you had more than one detention. Is that correct, Carrie?"

"Yes."

"How many?"

"I don't remember." I felt a little shiver run up and down my spine. A knot started to grow in my stomach.

"You don't remember. Well, I can help you. I see seven detentions listed. Seven, Carrie."

"Those were from Ms. Craddick and Mr. Fricter."

"And is it true that Ms. Kramer let you leave a detention set by Mr. Fricter before it was finished?"

"That's not true. We didn't deserve a detention."

"Are you *questioning* a teacher's aide giving a detention?" Ms. Thurman glared at me. "Isn't it true, Carrie, that you also received a detention because you and four other students were found talking behind the gym when you were supposed to have returned directly to class?"

I nodded.

Ms. Thurman stared at me with a cold smile.

"Now, I have a report here from Ms. Craddick that says that she had to keep reminding a couple students about the school rules from the very beginning of this last school year. And she noted that you were her biggest problem in the class. Does that surprise you, Carrie?"

I shook my head.

Ms. Thurman looked down at her note pad.

"Let's see here. Ahh yes. Ms. Craddick wrote, 'Student can't sit still. Student kicks her desk. Student scribbles pictures when she should be doing her work. Student needs to work harder and listen better.' I also see that your grades dropped this year, and that last year, your teacher noted ..." Ms. Thurman paused, shook her head and frowned as she looked at her notepad again. "'Student's attention deteriorated towards the end of the year. Student needed frequent reminders to sit still and concentrate. Student had four detentions for failing to complete work or getting out of her seat without permission.' What were you upset about last year, Carrie? Were you having trouble with your fourth-grade teacher as well as your fifth-grade teacher?"

Out of the corner of my eye, I saw Mr. Fricter smiling his crooked half-smile while Chad and Connor leaned forward in their chairs holding their fists up, like they were about to cheer their favorite baseball player as he rounded third base heading for home plate. I felt my heart racing and beating so loud I was afraid everyone could it hear it. I saw the school board members staring at me from the other side of the stage. I looked away from them and out into the gym. Rows and rows of adults I didn't know stared at me. They were all looking at me. I was all alone. No father. No mother.

They hate me, I thought. It wasn't fair. I kicked my foot and accidentally hit the table leg. The microphone fell over making another loud screech. I dove to pick it up. My hands shook as I put the microphone back in place.

Ms. Thurman shook her head and went on.

"And I see here a report from Mr. Fricter from the first week Ms. Kramer took over the class. 'Teacher encourages student, CS, who has gotten into repeated trouble'." Ms. Thurman looked again at me. "Is that you Carrie?" Then, she continued reading from Mr. Fricter's notes from a few days later. "'Teacher encourages student, CS, with multiple detentions to question teachers.'"

Ms. Thurman looked at the school board members sitting on either side of her.

"Sounds like Ms. Kramer was teaching her class to challenge teachers and other authorities."

I could see Mr. Fricter smiling broadly now. He was leaning back in his chair, his hands clasped across his protruding belly.

Ms. Thurman went on.

"And then, there was the fight in the cafeteria last week. The resource officer's report indicated that 'Student (CS) threw her tray with hot soup and spaghetti on one boy, repeatedly kicked that boy and slugged another boy. Student then kicked a cafeteria aide and a resource officer multiple times resulting in the security officer suffering minor injuries. Police were summoned. Student (CS) was suspended one day.

"'Kicking and hitting a fellow student. Kicking a cafeteria aide. Kicking a security officer over and over. Refusing to obey directions.'" Ms. Thurman shook her head slowly from side to side, and then glared suddenly at Principal Pratt. "Safety was jeopardized at Bartonsville Elementary. I really wonder if a one-day suspension was sufficient to protect our students."

Ms. Thurman frowned deeply and turned to her fellow school board members.

"We simply cannot allow violence in our school cafeterias. We need to restore discipline for education to work.

"Now," Ms. Thurman said, "we do like to hear from *all* of our students, no matter what they've done." She turned back towards me with a stiff little smile. Her eyes slammed so hard into me that I felt my head snap back. "Is there anything else you would like to say to the school board?"

I looked at the microphone. I felt tired, weak and small, like a little rat hiding from a cat, shivering in a corner of a cage, locked in with no escape. My stomach ached so bad I thought it would burst. I could hardly breathe, let alone speak to rows and rows of adults I didn't know. I felt their eyes staring at me, blaming me, hating me. My legs began kicking wildly. My head and shoulders sagged forward. I felt my hair drop over my face. My back started to ache. A teardrop grew in my right eye. I was afraid I would start to cry right in front of everyone. I tried to fight it. *Not now. Not ever! Not now. Not ever!* But the tears came anyway, streaking hot and wet, streaming down my face. I couldn't even see straight.

CHAPTER 22

Grandma's lesson

I heard the chair next to me sliding but I couldn't move. I felt frozen, shaking like a trapped little rat cowering before a large cat. I could hardly breathe. Hot wet tears streamed down my face.

I felt a hand gently stroke my back, slowly turning, round and round, in little circles. The hand gently loosened the knots in my back and warmed my body. Slowly, I felt my breath return and I turned my head. I peeked through my tear-soaked hair and saw Mom smiling back at me.

Mom wrapped her arms around me and hugged me tightly. I felt her heart beating along with mine, the two of us together, two hearts beating as one. The stage, the school board, all the other people faded away.

"I found your story in your dresser this morning when I put your socks away. I didn't know what to do after I read it. First, I got mad, mad at myself, thinking I'd failed once again. I let you down. Just like everyone else in my life since Grandma died. It just seemed like nothing worked any more. I didn't have anyone to talk to. And every time things went wrong, in my job, with your father, I got angrier. I kept thinking I had to do everything for someone else, a boss, your father, you, your brother. I guess that was easier than feeling I was failing, easier than thinking about doing what was right for myself, easier than thinking about how disappointed Grandma would have been to see what happened since she died, easier than thinking how I was driving your father away, easier than thinking about how I was letting you and Kevin down."

I saw a tear in my mother's right eye and then another in her left. I squeezed Mom tight and stopped fighting the tears running down my own face. I felt Mom's arms around me like a warm blanket as Mom whispered softly in my ear.

"All day long, I thought about your Dad. He would have been here, even if he had to drive all night." Mom sighed. Her face was wet with tears, like mine. "I'm so sorry Carrie. So sorry for what I did that night. And for what I haven't done since that night."

Mom sighed again. "The police officers told me Dad was driving home when the truck hit his car. He must have turned around. He was coming home. I think he heard you Carrie. He heard you call out to him to stay. He loved us too much to really leave. I always knew that. And I miss him so much."

Mom wiped her face and went on.

"And I kept thinking about what Grandma would have done. And then I realized I knew what Grandma would have done. I knew deep inside, in my heart. But, more than that, I knew what I wanted to do. I knew what I needed to do. And then," Mom took a deep breath, "and then, I knew I could do it too."

Mom looked into my eyes. She gently wiped away my tears. Then she pulled the microphone in front of her, keeping one arm wrapped around my shoulders. Mom turned towards the school board and began speaking in a soft voice that became stronger and stronger.

"I am very proud to be Carrie's mother. And I should have spoken out long ago. I watched my child lose interest in school in the last two years. I saw my child change from being excited about school to hating it. I thought, *maybe it's a phase. I'm sure the teachers know what's best.* But, really, to be honest, I was too busy with my own problems to do anything."

Mom looked into my eyes again and shook her head slowly.

"And I forgot what my own mother had taught me. 'There's nothing more important than raising children.' And that means being there for them when they need you, in good times and bad."

Mom looked again at me and nodded. Then, she turned back towards the School Board, speaking slowly now, her voice strong and clear.

"In these last three months, I saw my child transform back to the excellent student she used to be. She was excited again about learning. I'm not really sure what Ms. Kramer did, but I heard my daughter begin to ask questions again and search for answers. She became excited about learning."

Mom sighed.

"That meant asking questions that I didn't want to answer, questions I just hoped would go away. But, you know, the hard questions don't go away until we figure out what happened and do something to make things better. That means dealing with what happened and what's really going on. And when parents are too busy, or too afraid, and when teachers, like Ms. Craddick, tell children to not ask questions, 'just listen.' Well, there's no learning."

Mom sighed and looked at the school board members.

"I'm not saying I have the answers about creating the best fifth grade curriculum. But I know one thing. Ms. Kramer engaged our children in real learning. I'm grateful to Ms. Kramer for being my daughter's teacher."

Mom turned and smiled at me.

"And I'm grateful to my daughter for opening my eyes to what matters the most."

Ms. Thurman glared at Mom long and hard. Then she drilled her eyes into me. This time, though, I just stared right back, long and hard, straight into Ms. Thurman's eyes. I felt Mom's arm around my shoulders. Ms. Thurman had no power over me now.

The whole gym was strangely quiet like everybody was waiting for something to happen. Ms. Thurman opened her mouth and looked like she was about to launch into another series of biting questions directed at Mom and me. I could see her teeth and her tongue start to move. Her eyes darted back and forth between Mom and me, then she stared hard at Mom. But Mom just stared right back at her, eye to eye. It was like a pitcher and a batter, checking each other out with the count '3 and 2'.

Ms. Thurman didn't say a word. After a couple minutes, I reached for Mom's hand. We left the stage and found seats near my friends.

Principal Pratt stepped up on the stage and sat down at the small table.

"I taught elementary school for 20 years before becoming a principal. I've learned that having a good curriculum is important. But, it's *not* enough. The idea of a teacher standing up in front of a class and drumming facts and skills into students simply doesn't work.

"Watching what happened in Classroom 5D reminded me of what teaching is all about. The most successful teachers create a relationship with each student and engage their students to explore and discover the magic inside Math, Social Studies, Literary Arts and Science.

"What works in fifth grade?" Principal Pratt asked. She picked up a stack of papers.

"I have 22 papers here. Papers that students in Ms. Kramer's classroom wrote about how heroes get past their fears to help others. Twenty-two papers from students who were told by their teacher's aide that they shouldn't turn in this homework assignment. But, 22 out of 24 students completed these papers anyway. These 22 students were so inspired that they wanted to continue learning even after their teacher was suspended."

Principal Pratt looked at the school board.

"That's quite a tribute to their teacher, Ms. Kramer, and a message to all of us in administration about what works."

"I read these papers and I was inspired myself. Some students wrote about getting over fears of snakes or spiders or standing on high places. Others wrote about how they learned to step back and see scary things from a distance, and then huge fears became smaller and smaller until they could be managed. One student wrote, 'The hard part is seeing what's going on when you're feeling small, when what you fear looks so huge and powerful that you feel you can't escape. That's when it's easy to go crazy, to freeze, and to stop looking for answers. And that's when you can learn from heroes how to get safe again.' This student wrote that what helped her get past her fears were her memories about her family loving each other, her friends, and a brave teacher who risked her job to help her students learn.

"For this student and the other 22 students who brought their papers to me, something wonderful happened over the last three months in Classroom 5D. It was like the class came out of a deep and disturbed sleep. I'm going to recommend that other fifth-grade teachers use the same approach next year."

Ms. Thurman looked like she was going to jump out of her chair.

"What about the reports that Ms. Kramer did not allow sufficient time for students to learn the core subjects of our curriculum, that Ms. Kramer did not prepare her students for the state-wide fifth grade exams?"

"I found that all the subjects were covered. And, even more important, students showed they could use the skills they learned in all core subjects."

"What about Ms. Kramer reducing the detention of three students who violated school rules?"

"That was entirely appropriate once the facts were known. I also found that Ms. Kramer's putting two boys in detention for breaking class rules was appropriate under the school's guidelines, and, if anything, their penalties should have been far greater given how they violated school codes regarding theft and how they hurt other students."

Ms. Thurman clutched her microphone. Her voice boomed through the speakers.

"What about the diseased rodent who was loose in the classroom endangering the health of our students?"

"That little rat was never loose or diseased or a danger to our students," Principal Pratt said, "that I know." She went on to describe how Cami and Crystal had found the rat in a dumpster behind the school and how the veterinarian at the Animal Hospital said that the little rat had been bruised, squeezed hard by small child-size fingers.

"How do you know those two girls didn't put the rat in the dumpster? How do *you* know *they* didn't squeeze the rat and then try to claim credit for saving it?" Ms. Thurman glared again at Principal Pratt.

"What I know," Principal Pratt said, staring steadily back with a clear, calm voice, "is that all the little rats were okay before the students went to gym class, lunch, and a special program that day. And during that time, students, including Cami and Crystal, were marked in attendance for gym, lunch, and the special program. Two students, however, missed gym and didn't return until the end of the special program that day."

"But you don't have any evidence that those two students put the rat in the dumpster."

"No, but we do know that these were the same two boys who were unhappy about getting detentions from Ms. Kramer."

"But did anybody see them? Shouldn't administrators be a little more careful before making allegations of misconduct, Ms. Pratt?"

"I saw them," a man called out. Mr. Cook stood up. He had been sitting in the back row of the gym. "I was taking out the cafeteria garbage when I noticed two students walking away from one of the trash bins. I said, 'Aren't you supposed to be in class?' and they said 'Yes, sir. We just got back from doctors' appointments.' Then, one of them pretended to cough. You could tell he was faking it. The other one laughed. I followed them to the gym and made sure they joined their class."

"Can you identify those two students?" Ms. Thurman asked, glaring now at Carrie and her friends.

"Sure can. They were on the bus I used to drive. Chad and Connor. I remember those two boys very well. Yes, I do. Had to keep them in line and in their seats many times. Always seemed to be poking some other child or doing something they shouldn't to other students. They needed a constant eye on them, those two boys."

Ms. Thurman frowned deeply.

"Well this doesn't answer the question about how to run a fifth-grade classroom, or the complaints about Ms. Kramer's teaching. And, clearly, not every student in the class liked how Ms. Kramer was teaching. What about the two students who didn't turn in their Heroes papers?"

"Yes, that's a good point," Principal Pratt said. "Those two students are going to need a lot of extra help. There are laws about abusing animals and stealing school property. This will have to be reported to the authorities. We are also waiting for a review of the videos from the cafeteria the day of the fight last week to find out what really happened. There are rules to keep everyone safe everywhere in our school. And they will be enforced."

Ms. Thurman turned to look at Chad and Connor. Now, everyone was staring at them. Connor's father's face was red. His eyes were cold and his mouth looked like he was about to bite someone's head off. It was the same look I'd seen a hundred times on Connor's face when he attacked another boy or girl. Suddenly, Connor's father grabbed Connor by the back of his shirt collar and yanked him out of his chair so hard he almost knocked Connor's chair over. Then, he shoved Connor ahead of him and out of the gym. Connor's mother followed behind, looking down and shaking her head. Chad's mother pushed Chad along right behind them. She shoved Chad so hard he almost fell over.

I saw Connor drop his sweet, angelic look. His face showed nothing now but terror. His mask was gone. Connor winced when his father shoved him a second time. Chad looked like he was about to cry.

165

Principal Pratt returned to her seat. Several adults lined up to speak.

David's grandfather recalled how he and his wife had sent their children and now their grandson to Bartonsville Elementary.

"I told my grandson this was a great school, how it had been a good school for his father. But privately I had been worried about some of the things I had heard from friends and neighbors. We were relieved when we met Ms. Kramer and very pleased with the changes Ms. Kramer brought to the class. She showed her students that reading, writing, math, science, and social studies can be important in their lives. She's been wonderful for our grandson and we thank Principal Pratt for hiring her."

Crystal's mother talked about how she hoped Ms. Kramer would come back soon and how Ms. Kramer brought out the best in her daughter. Then, Theresa's mother walked up to the table.

"I was scared," she said, "scared about the little rats, about rats biting my child. I want to thank Principal Pratt for finding out what happened. I'm not worried anymore."

Cami's father talked about how bored Cami had been and how she started to like school again after Ms. Kramer came. Four other parents followed Cami's father. They talked about how their children didn't seem to be learning anything until Ms. Kramer came.

As each parent spoke, Ms. Thurman's frown grew deeper and deeper.

"Any other comments?" she asked with a muffled voice. She kept looking at the door of the gym like she wanted to get away as fast as possible.

"Okay," Ms. Thurman started to say. "If there are no other comments …"

An elderly man sitting to her left, one of the school board members, pulled over the microphone she had been using. Ms. Thurman looked again at the closed gym doors.

"Thank you, parents. Thank you, students," the man said and looked at me. "And, Carrie, thank you for speaking up, young lady. I too have watched changes in our elementary schools. I've been watching for the last 30 years and I haven't liked a lot of what I have seen."

The elderly man turned toward the school board president who was now slumped in her chair.

"I want to thank Ms. Thurman for bringing us to Bartonsville Elementary today. I think I've seen enough to know that something has happened this spring in Classroom 5D, something happened that brought back real learning. So, I join with our last speaker in saying, 'Thank you, Principal Pratt.'"

A woman sitting to the right of Ms. Thurman took the microphone.

"I make a motion to compliment Principal Pratt and Classroom 5D," she said.

"I second that," a man said from the end of the table.

Everyone turned toward Ms. Thurman who seemed to be staring at the gym door with glassy eyes and a blank look on her face.

"Let's have a vote then," she finally said in a faint voice. "All in favor?"

All of the school board members raised their hands except Ms. Thurman.

"The motion carries. This meeting is adjourned. The board will move to the teacher's conference room for our closed meeting on Ms. Kramer and Principal Pratt."

Mom wrapped her arms around me.

"You were wonderful," Mom said. "Dad would have been really proud of you. Grandma would have told all her friends how brave you were." Mom smiled. It was Mom's old smile, the smile I had been missing so much, the smile that told me everything would be okay.

I looked up at Mom.

"I told them about what wasn't being said. Uncle Phil told me that's what Dad would have done. And my friends and I got the kids in our class to turn in their Heroes papers to Principal Pratt."

"Brilliant. I'm so proud of you." Mom pulled me close and hugged me again, a deep-warm Mom-hug, the kind I had been missing so much.

Cami, Crystal, and David came running over.

"Awesome!" David said. "You hit it out of the park."

"Classy and cool," Crystal said smiling.

Cami hugged me.

"And now we know what really happened with Ms. Craddick. I heard one of the school board members say she was in trouble all along with Principal Pratt. She was about to be replaced because she had so much trouble teaching. That's why she left."

I hugged my friends. Then the four of us started walking toward the door.

I looked behind me as we left the gym. Mom, David's grand-parents, Cami's father, and Crystal's mother were walking to-gether. Mom was smiling. I knew we both wished Dad was with us. But there was a light in her eyes that I had missed so much.

My heart started to soar for just a second, then fell back into place. We couldn't go back to the way we were, Mom, Dad, Kevin, and me. But I could see something else. We could go on, loving each other, even though we missed Dad so much. I felt my head start to nod. I started to smile, just a little smile. But it was a real smile, a smile that warmed my whole body. I turned and grabbed Cami's hand on one side and Crystal's hand on the other.

"Friends forever," I said and Cami, Crystal and David joined in, "Stick together!"

Then, just for fun, we ran down the hall, out the school door and into the sunshine.

CHAPTER 23
The new banner

Mom, my friends, their parents, David's grandparents and I waited outside to find out what would be decided at the private school board meeting about Principal Pratt. We didn't have to wait long. The meeting didn't last more than a few minutes. Ms. Thurman walked out of the school building frowning with her head down, not looking at anyone. Then, Principal Pratt stepped out and saw my friends and me.

"See you in class tomorrow," Principal Pratt said with a smile. It was the first time I had ever seen her smile. Her eyes seemed to twinkle. She looked ten years younger.

The rest of the school year flew by and ended way too soon. Mr. Fricter decided he'd had enough with troublesome students and left to take another job. Ms. Kramer returned to the class and asked us to work on one last Heroes paper. She asked the class to write a paper that would be shared with future fifth-grade students about what each student had learned was most important to help people get through hard times and make things better for themselves and their families.

Ms. Kramer added a special question that she asked me to include in my paper.

"You said, the first day I met you that heroes tell the truth. What did you learn was the truth from your heroes?"

I thought about everything that had happened since Ms. Kramer came to Classroom 5D and the hard times before.

"I learned that the truth can get lost in tough times," I said. "Tough times are sort of like prickers and vines. They can grow and grow and snake around trees and homes and everything. And before you know it, they cover up what's beautiful so much that you can't see the good things or remember the fun times or the people who loved you. All you see are dark, tangled vines, everywhere, like prickly ropes trapping everybody. But, if you're brave enough, and if you get help, you can cut through the vines and find the truth."

"And what did you find?"

"I thought I was the only one in my family who cared anymore. But the truth was that my mom really cared. My dad had really cared. Even, my little brother tried his best."

"And I've learned a lot too," Ms. Kramer said smiling at me, "about the courage of students who dare to speak up."

On the last day of school, Principal Pratt had the entire school come down to the gym. She thanked all the teachers and all the students for their hard work this last year. Then, she asked Mr. Cook to come up to the stage.

"I'd like to thank the students of Classroom 5D and Ms. Kramer for inspiring our new school banner."

Then, she and Mr. Cook unrolled the banner, and together, they lifted it up. The banner read:

Bartonsville Elementary

Heroes Welcome

Principal Pratt smiled and looked at me as the students cheered. I looked at my friends. Then, I noticed something very strange. I was smiling and not just a little smile. It was my old smile. The My mask was gone.

Epilogue

That was the end of my fifth-grade year. I know I was lucky. Since then, I have wondered what would have happened if Mom had not come to the school board meeting. What if she had not read my letter? What if she had been too scared to ask for time away from her new job? What if Mom had been too worn down to do anything? What if she had given up trying to make things better?

I felt all alone up on that stage. I thought I had lost Dad, Grandma, Mom, Ms. Kramer, everyone I needed. I blamed myself for failing to keep Dad home. My school record was full of detentions and teacher notes. The school board president was telling everyone how terrible I was. And, worse than that, I was starting to believe her.

This story could have had a very different ending, a harder ending. Dad was dead. I can say that out loud now. I still cry when I think of him. But I don't block it away. I don't go nuts any more trying not to remember Dad or what happened. I keep in my heart how much he loved Kevin, Mom and me. I remember the love that turned him around to come home that terrible night. And I know now that Mom would have still cared, even if she had not found a way to be there with me on that stage.

I didn't know all that back when I was 11. Now that I am older, I know I could still have remembered Mom's hugs from when I was younger and how hard she tried every day working for our family. I could have remembered the good things she saw in me and how much she wanted for me. That would have helped me go on and not give up.

Now that I am older, I also know there were other people who cared and other people who were strong. I know how much Grandma loved me and the strength she instilled inside Mom and me. Mom still calls me 'Carrie' but outside of home I go by Caroline now, the name my grandmother picked for me. Thinking of Grandma helps me become stronger.

I hope you are lucky enough to have a grandma like I had, or a grandpa, an aunt, uncle, older brother or sister, or a cousin who cares about you, even if your parents can't. I hope you have friends like Cami, Crystal, or David. I hope you know teachers like Ms. Kramer or a principal like Ms. Pratt. I hope you have neighbors like the Cohen's.

It helps me to think of all these people. It helps me to know that there are a lot of people who care enough to do something even when it means taking risks. There are a lot of people who are strong enough to tell the truth. Those people are my heroes.

Like I said, I was lucky. After fifth grade ended, Mom, Kevin and I learned to smile and have good times again and I knew Mom would always be there for me when I needed her. David went back to live with his parents. As for Cami, Crystal and me, there would be other mysteries to solve and hard times to make better. We were just beginning ...

Behind the Mask: Secrets of Real Life Heroes by Carrie Sanderson

These are some of the things I learned this year about what helps girls and boys, men and women, to be brave in 'tough times.'

Dare to learn.

It takes more than courage to be a hero. Heroes have to be smart but they aren't born that way. They have to learn how to figure things out. They ask questions even when people tell them to stop asking and just believe what they are told. They dare to learn what some people may be too afraid to find out, like a trick soccer kick that everybody says is impossible. And they keep learning, even if they fall on their faces or other people laugh at them.

Find people who can help you.

When you're having trouble, it's easy to blame yourself and to think no one cares enough to help. It's hard to be brave when you feel you are all alone. That's when you really need your friends and your family and other people like teachers who really care. Finding out who cares can be the hardest thing to do.

Find out what is real.

Telling the truth is hard. It's a lot easier to pretend. Some people think that pretending is for kids, but the truth is that people get better and better at pretending the older they get. And sometimes, they get so good at pretending, they forget what's real.

Don't be afraid to look behind the masks people wear.

In some stories, people are afraid to see what's under a monster's mask. But, it's really the monster's mask that keeps us scared. Behind the mask, you can see what the monster is really like, even what the monster is scared about. Then, you can find a way to become safe again.

When people wear masks, the good things about those people get covered up along with their real faces, like how people care and how people want to help. When people wear masks all the time, no one finds out what is really true and what is just a scary story. Everyone stays scared.

Know how your own mask works.

Superheroes from comic books or movies, like Batman or Spiderman, wore masks so no one would know who they really were. That helped protect them and the people they cared about. But, that's just part of the story. Sometimes heroes wear masks because everyone around them is wearing a mask too. The difference is that heroes know why they are wearing their masks. Heroes learn how their masks work. And heroes can take their masks off.

Heroes have problems.

My dad was a hero. My Mom is a hero too. But they were never perfect. No one is. My mom showed me that real heroes can own what they did wrong and make things better.

Find out what really happened.

People sometimes learn to never ask questions so they won't upset people they care about. People can get so used to not asking questions that no one tries to find out what really happened. And, if you never find out what happened, you can never know how to make things better.

Real heroes help us go behind the masks that hide what happened. Heroes help us find out what is real and work to make things better, even when asking questions means that you might get in trouble with people who are afraid to learn the truth.

Don't ever give up.

Some people say *trying to make things better* means you are acting *bold* or *rude*. But, I think *trying to make things better* is a tiny voice inside you, a voice that says that it's better to find out what's real than hide behind a mask forever. It's a belief that something can change for the better and that the worst thing is feeling stuck or giving up.

It's worth trying to make things better, even if you don't get what you really want.

If one person tries, it helps other people try too. If you give up, hope dies. Trying keeps hope alive.

Heroes care.

Heroes aren't afraid to show they care. Heroes care enough to ask questions other people are afraid to ask. They care enough to say things other people don't dare to say. They care enough to help the people they love become safe enough and strong enough to take off their masks.

Note from the author

In my work as a clinical psychologist, children have shared with me traumatic experiences that ripped their families apart and shattered their sense of trust and belonging. These same children have also shared with me a yearning to be loved and the courage to change. I have been inspired by how children recovered from losses of the family members they loved, emotional, physical and sexual abuse, family violence, neglect, and abandonments. I have also seen how many children remained mired in the nightmares of their lives and appeared to relive their greatest fears day after day. Many children appeared cut off from emotionally supportive relationships with caring adults and appeared to repeat the abuse and violence they had experienced in their own behaviors. Dangerous behaviors led to referrals to child welfare services, juvenile justice programs, psychiatric hospitals or behavioral health care programs.

My job as a psychologist was to engage these children and their families and to find a way to understand what had happened and what could be done to help them. Rather than viewing these children as helpless victims or frightening aggressors, I learned to listen and watch for clues to what made these children smile as well as what led to dangerous behaviors. From these children, their parents, caregivers, and my colleagues, I learned lessons about what could be done to transform their lives. I also learned how their stories of trauma and recovery could inspire all of us.

Each child and family I have worked with has taught me a lesson of how ordinary people can rise up to surmount tragedies. Very often, the worst traumas involved the breakdown of a child's trust in parents, guardians, and other adults to keep themselves and their families safe. Many children appeared cut off from emotionally supportive relationships with caring adults and appeared to repeat the abuse and violence they had experienced in their own behaviors. Parents, grandparents, teachers, counselors and other caring adults often felt threatened by what children did and said after multiple traumas. Caring adults often felt disempowered and unable to re-connect with troubled children. At the same time, troubled children often felt increasingly alone and desperate with little hope.

I wrote *The Hero's Mask* to create openings for parents, teachers, therapists, and other caring adults to encourage children to share what may be hidden from adults—what makes them smile, what they yearn for, who they admire, and what drives their fears. Children read stories and connect with feelings of characters like themselves facing real-life problems like the death of a parent, parents' fighting, financial problems, or school bullies. And these stories of facing and overcoming problems can, in turn, renew hope and bring out children's drive to learn skills and make things better. In the same way, books can remind adults how they can become the heroes children need to face unspoken terrors and to learn to grow and thrive again after experiencing adversity. In this way, books like *The Hero's Mask* can help children and caring adults repair frayed bonds and recover from losses and other stressful experiences.

Helping Children with Traumatic Stress; The Hero's Mask Guidebook for Parents, Caregivers, Educators, Counselors and Therapists[1] includes suggestions and guidelines for how parents, caregivers, educators, counselors and therapists can use *The Hero's Mask* novel to help the children they love. The *Guidebook* also includes resources and re-ferences to find additional information about helping children and families with traumatic stress and use of *Real Life Heroes*® *(RLH)*, an evidence-supported treatment program for children and families with traumatic stress. *The Real Life Heroes Toolkit for Treating Traumatic stress in Children and Families*, 2nd Edn. (Routledge, 2017), *The Real Life Heroes Life Storybook*, 3rd Edn. (Routledge, 2017) and *Rebuilding Attachments with Traumatized Children* (Routledge, 2004) provide an integrated framework for use of RLH in resiliency-focused treatment for traumatic stress and development of trauma-informed schools and treatment programs.[2] *The Hero's Mask* and RLH books can be used in to promote an understanding of trauma

and to strengthen (or develop) attunement and emotionally supportive relationships between children and caring adults and resilience to traumatic stress in families, schools and communities.

Richard Kagan
February 29, 2020

Notes

1 Kagan, R. (2020). *Helping Children with Traumatic Stress: The Hero's Mask
   Guidebook for Parents, Caregivers, Educators, Counselors and Therapists*.
   New York: Routledge.
2 For stories of children with traumatic stress and the lessons they can
   teach us, please see: *Wounded Angels, Inspiration from Children in Crisis*
   (Routledge, 2017). For additional information about *Real Life Heroes*®,
   please see www.reallifeheroes.net.

About the author

Dr. Kagan provides training and consultation on traumatic stress and complex trauma treatment and is an affiliate member of the National Child Traumatic Stress Network (NCTSN). He has had leadership experience in child and family services as the director of professional development, QI, research, and psychological services for Parsons Child and Family Center, a NCTSN community services site since 2002, and served as the principal investigator for two SAMHSA-funded NCTSN grants and as the Director of Research and Consultation for the Sidney Albert Training and Research Institute. Dr. Kagan co-led development of the NCTSN curriculum, *Caring for Children Who Have Experienced Traumatic Stress* as co-chair of the Resource Parent Committee and served on the NCTSN Steering Committee, the NCTSN Affiliate Advisory Group, the Complex Trauma and Child Welfare Committees and the advisory group for development of the NCTSN's Trauma-Informed Organizational Assessment.

Dr. Kagan's presentations, articles, and books highlight practical and innovative approaches that practitioners and organizations can utilize to help children and families strengthen resilience and reduce traumatic stress. Dr. Kagan's publications include 35+ articles and papers on practice and research issues in trauma therapy, child welfare, foster care, adoption, training implementation, program evaluation, and quality improvement and 12 books including *The Real Life Heroes Toolkit for Treating Traumatic Stress in Children and Families, The Real Life Heroes Life Storybook, Rebuilding Attachments with Traumatized Children* and *Wounded Angels; Inspiration from Children in Crisis*. Further information about Dr. Kagan's publications, training programs and professional experience can be found at www.reallifeheroes.net.